Gateways to Growth and Maturity

Through the Life of Esther

Penny Smith
Foreword by Wade Taylor

McDougal Publishing is a ministry of The McDougal Foundation, Inc., a Maryland nonprofit corporation dedicated to spreading the Gospel of the Lord Jesus Christ to as many people as possible in the shortest time possible.

Published by:
Mcdougal Publishing
P.O. Box 3595
Hagerstown, MD 21742-3595
www.mcdougalpublishing.com

ISBN 1-58158-094-0

Printed in the United States of America
For Worldwide Distribution

Foreword

This book, *Gateways to Growth and Maturity* is not for those who are faint of heart; nor is it for those who have made only a casual commitment to the Lord, and are satisfied.

It is however, a book that will awaken the reader to a deeper sense of spiritual need, indeed, a divinely initiated desire to walk closer with the Lord. As the writer examines the book of Esther in the light of both Old and New Testament Scriptures, its hidden gems are uncovered, and mysteries unveiled, by the redemptive work of the Cross. The writer also employs practical applications of Scripture, as well as inspirational vignettes, to solidify principles and practical truths gleaned from Esther's story. As we journey with Esther from her beginnings as a simple Jewish girl to her promotion as queen, and ultimately to her destined vocation as deliverer to her people, the author continually draws our attention to the various levels of maturity through which Esther must pass in order to fulfill the purpose and mandate upon her life.

We too must be willing to walk through the gateways that have been set before us, if we are to recognize, and fully respond to our Lord's call.

Gateways to Growth and Maturity is a book for those who both desire and intend to rise to the challenge of becoming a part of a Kingdom body of believers, made ready for such a time as this.

Wade E. Taylor

Preface

The book of Esther contains spiritual truths that may not be readily apparent on the surface. All Scripture is given by inspiration of God, so in many instances there are messages which we do not receive simply because we become entrapped in a quest for knowledge by reviewing and discussing facts, making our analyses, engaging in doctrinal disputes, and generally reading and studying to discover reasons for this and that, rather than allowing the Holy Spirit to impart a deeper truth.

There is nothing wrong with approaching the Scriptures in the above fashion; but Jesus said, "*Search the Scriptures; for in them ye think ye have eternal life: and they are they which testify of Me*" (John 5:39). Thus, my approach is to engage us in a search for Him, that One of whom the Scriptures speak.

The book of Esther is a book for today. It offers for the Bride of Christ lessons and insights into the greater blessings given to those of purer faith. It shows a clear path to the overcoming Christian experience. Its gems are hidden, veiled, even buried beneath the form of the writing. Yet there is a pattern of spiritual truths that emerges when we compare parallel passages found throughout the Scriptures.

For the purposes of this study, which will be devotional and inspirational in nature, we prayerfully launch out into the depths of His message to our hearts.

Lord, speak to the hearts of those who long to know You more intimately. Grant to each a clearer understanding of Your purposes in the earth today, and that together we may please You and bring honor to Your Name.

Acknowledgments

Shortly before the Lord opened the truths of Esther to me in a new way, He placed in my hands a book that in many ways led to the inspiration of this one. I would be remiss should I fail to mention and highly recommend *The Secret Of The Stairs,* authored by Wade E. Taylor of Pinecrest Publications, Salisbury Center, New York.

To Agape Fellowship in Christ, Harrisburg, Pennsylvania, who, under the pastorate of Thomas and Mary Mellott, sponsored the radio program *Gateways to Growth,* on which this series of messages on the book of Esther was birthed.

To Dawn Edmondson, to whom the first edition was dedicated, for being my sounding board through its original birth pangs.

To my friend and writing mentor, Anne Lorimer Sirna, I apologize for all the rules I may have broken in my first attempt. I trust some improvements have been made in this edition.

To my family and the many friends who believe in me more than I believe in myself.

To the memory of one so richly endowed with God's graces, and to whom I owe my spiritual heritage and, hopefully, impartation, "Dad Butler."

More recently, to Tina Luce, whose encouragement with the Gateways CD project has led to the republishing of this work.

And to Janet Durbin at McDougal Publishing, who expressed the belief that this is the appointed time for the publication of this book.

Contents

Introduction

The book of Esther, unlike the other books of the Bible, is written in secular style and its author is unknown. Although the two principal characters of the book, Esther and Mordecai, are of Jewish origin, the *name* of God is not once mentioned, nor is there reference to the Levitical system of sacrifice. Yet it cannot be denied that He is uniquely present in the lives of His chosen ones.

The book of Esther itself is named for Esther the Jewess, who was raised to the rank of queen, to whom the Jews were indebted for their deliverance from threatened destruction. With the help of the Holy Spirit, we will learn why this young woman became the king's favorite, so much so that he granted her every request; and we shall appreciate the source of Esther's courage as she overcame her personal weaknesses.

Some have set forth the characters in the book of Esther as types, but this writer chose rather to present parallel truths and suggested symbolisms, comparing scripture with scripture and noting contrasts between Esther's kingdom and the one to which we belong, the Kingdom of our Lord and of His Christ.

It is generally agreed that King Ahasuerus of the book of Esther was most likely the Persian king Xerxes I, who was known in history as being extravagant, fickle, and unstable. The king in our text reigned at least twelve years during a period when the Persians had preeminence over the Medes.

Esther and her cousin, Mordecai, were of the tribe of Benjamin. Mordecai is said to have been the great-grandson of Jehoiachin, who, with many of the people including Ezekiel, was taken to Babylon 120 years before Esther was made queen.

It has often been noted that the book of Esther is a striking counterpart to the books of Ezra and Nehemiah, both of which show the favor of God upon the exiles who returned to the holy city for its rebuilding and restoration. But Esther shows the character of many Jews who did not choose to return to the holy city from exile. It further substantiates that although multitudes preferred the lands of exile to the land of Israel, they were obviously not without Jehovah's oversight and care.

This may be a comforting thought to those who have not yet discovered the pathway to a victorious Christian experience. But I trust that by the time you complete this study each of us will yearn for and actively seek a relationship with our Lord and King that will compare to Queen Esther's position in the courts of the king she served.

It will be our *gateway to growth and maturity.*

1

Treasures

Esther 1:1-5

*He showed the riches of his glorious kingdom and the honor
of his excellent majesty.*   Esther 1:4

King Ahasuerus (whose name has numerous spellings
and pronunciations), of Persia, in the third year of his
reign, gave a feast for certain notable persons of his kingdom at Susa.

Some of the facts about him, according to the open-
ing chapter of Esther, are that his royal residence was in
Susa (or Shushan), the capital of the Persian Empire; his
dominion extended "from India even unto Ethiopia"
(we know that the borders are different today), and it
was the third year of his reign.

For some reason the king, over a period of 180 days,
had been displaying the splendor of his kingdom to all
the nobles and officers of his provinces. It was like a six-
month open house. At the completion of these days, the

king held a seven-day banquet for everyone in the capital of Susa.

It was quite a spread, served in the court of the garden of the king's palace.

The Jews and the Persians who were in Susa at the time had opportunity to see the exquisite beauty of the king's court. Even the children were invited. None would have guessed the empire was in a period of decline.

For he showed the riches of his glorious kingdom and the honor of his excellent majesty....

Let's make a few comparisons.

What can we say about our King, those of us who have become subjects of the Kingdom of God?

First, His royal residence is in Heaven, and yet, miracle of miracles, in the new birth He comes to abide within each individual who will receive Him.

His domain is the universe. The clouds are His chariots, His enemies are His footstool, and although we are as grasshoppers in His sight, He chose to identify with us in the mystery of God in the flesh.

His reign is from everlasting to everlasting. He is the Alpha and the Omega, the Beginning and the End, the First and the Last. He has overcome hell, death, and the grave. He has conquered Satan; and He has done so that we might live victorious Christian lives in Him.

Furthermore, we serve a King who is our heavenly Bridegroom. He desires to unveil our spiritual eyes for He too wants us to see *the riches of His glorious Kingdom, and the honor of His excellent majesty.* Our King desires neither to hide His ways nor to hoard His resources, but rather He delights to show us what lies within our spiritual storehouse.

The day will come when, as born-again children of God, we will be ushered into this glorious realm in a physical sense. John wrote about it in Revelation, and gave us a mere glimpse of those glories.

One of the seven angels of Revelation talked with John, saying, "*Come here, I shall show you the bride, the wife of the Lamb*" (Revelation 21:9, NASB). We know the Lamb is none other than Jesus Christ, "*the Lamb slain before the foundation of the world.*" John said he was carried away in the Spirit, and shown, the holy city Jerusalem. This city, called the bride, shone with the glory of God, for she descended out of heaven from God (see Revelation 21:10).

You may recall the description of King Solomon's temple, which he built for the Lord. It was grand, elaborate. We know that when the ark was carried into the Most Holy Place once again, the priests could not stand to minister because of the glory cloud which filled the house, as it did over the Tent of Meeting where Moses met with God.

The ark represented the presence of God.

And there I will meet with thee, and I will commune with thee from above the mercy seat, from between the two cherubim which are upon the ark of the testimony.

Exodus 25:22

He showed the honor of His excellent majesty.

He revealed His glory.

These cannot compare "*with the glory which shall be revealed in us*" (Romans 8:18). Our King is preparing a feast for us because He is getting ready to reveal His glory and His majesty to all, even to those of lesser faith.

> *The king made a feast unto all the people that were present*
> *in Shushan the palace, both unto great and small.*
>
> Esther 1:5

We are being prepared, the Bride who will appear from behind the scenes for the whole world to behold. Yet before His glorious Bride is revealed, she must first pass through days of purification during which she learns to please her heavenly Bridegroom *at any cost.*

It is this process which unveils the Revealer until that which she has not seen with her physical eyes becomes more real to her than that which she may handle.

The reality of the manifestation, the disclosure, of the presence of God is not to be confused with mysticism. However, many have missed walking in the deeper realm of spiritual revelation because of misconceptions about the presence of God. He has treasures to show us, and He will not give what we do not desire.

When the Lord reveals Himself, we will *know* Him. Isaiah declared, "*For the earth will be full of the knowledge of the* LORD *as the waters cover the sea*" (Isaiah 11:9, NASB). Our King desires to *show* us His treasures, but how can we be sure we will be among those who see?

We read,

> *The Kingdom of heaven is like unto treasure hid in a field;*
> *the which when a man hath found, he hideth, and for joy*
> *thereof goeth and selleth all that he hath, and buyeth that*

field. Again, the kingdom of heaven is like unto a merchantman, seeking goodly pearls: who, when he had found one pearl of great price, went and sold all that he had, and bought it.   Matthew 13:44-46

The question is, how much is it worth to us?

The apostle Paul said, "*We have this treasure in earthen vessels*" (2 Corinthians 4:7). Why, then, should we grovel in superficialities? According to Colossians 1:9, we are to "*be filled with the knowledge of His will in all wisdom and spiritual understanding.*"

Treasures, spiritual treasures. Treasures that are hidden in Christ.

But how do we tap into them?

In the Old Testament we have the account of Joseph, who was sold into slavery by his own brothers. They had thrown him into a pit and left him there to die, then decided instead to sell him into slavery. After all, they must not have their brother's death upon their consciences!

Joseph certainly had no idea that he would one day occupy a place of authority over the land of Egypt, where his brothers would bow to him and owe to him their lives. But the gateway to Joseph's kingdom was suffering, rejection, and the pain of separation.

The New Testament reveals a Man, beaten and weary, carrying His cross, stumbling beneath the load. When He hung upon that cross on a hill called Calvary, suspended between Heaven and hell, the demons danced with glee as the Man's Father turned His face from Him. Darkness covered the sky, the earth shook, and His followers fled from the sight of Him. Angels trembled when they heard the Man's anguished cry as the stroke of God's judgment fell upon Him for sins He had not committed.

My God, My God, why hast Thou forsaken Me?
                                                                                   Matthew 27:46

THE CROSS IS THE GATEWAY TO HIS GLORIOUS KINGDOM.

When we cannot reconcile our Christian experience with our sufferings, our failures, and our troubles; when the deep gnawing within finds no satisfaction; when a divine restlessness grips our hearts, we need to consider once again the Cross. Our King desires to show us the riches of His glorious Kingdom and the honor of His excellent majesty.

He desires to turn our water into wine.

2

Vessels of Gold

Esther 1:5-8

And they gave them drink in vessels of gold, (the vessels being diverse one from another,) and royal wine in abundance, according to the state of the king.   Esther 1:7

Now that the king had shown his treasures, the feast was prepared and would go on for seven days. It was for all the people, *"both great and small."* In God's Kingdom there is no such thing as a middle-class American. God does not care whether we wear a white collar, a blue collar, a turned-backwards collar, or no collar.

Whosoever will may come.

The invitation has gone out to the doctors and lawyers, the teachers and homemakers, the truckers and farmers, the plumbers and carpenters, the soldiers and merchants, the laborers and secretaries and especially to the unemployed. He calls *"the poor, the maimed, the lame,* [and] *the blind"* (Luke 14:13); and from a spiritual standpoint, that covers us all.

When Jesus gave the parable of the great supper, He pointedly said, "*None of those men which were bidden shall taste of My supper*" (Luke 14:24). Many are called, *but few are chosen.*

Who are the chosen, the qualified?

Jesus describes them as the cross-bearers, those who have counted the cost and have forsaken all to follow Him.

Who will respond?

Who will see the truths He is trying to disclose to His Bride?

> *The king gave a banquet...for all the people who were present ..., in the court of the garden of the king's palace.*
> Esther 1:5, NASB

In order to understand "the garden of the king's palace," we turn to several of the gardens mentioned in Scripture. The first of these, the Garden of Eden, was tended by Adam and Eve, who were given access to all that was in the garden, with the exception of the tree of the knowledge of good and evil. They were not to eat of that tree. They disobeyed, and as a result all creation stands under the curse of their disobedience. Jesus was born to redeem mankind from that curse. The Scriptures teach that without the shedding of blood there is no remission of sin (see Hebrews 9:22). Thus, Jesus shed His precious blood for our sin, making it possible for us *to enter the King's courts.*

Every child of God has had the Eden experience, the

sense of need and the acknowledgement of personal sin. Adam and Eve used fig leaves to cover their nakedness. We tried to cover the nakedness of sin with good deeds and resolutions, but found them flimsy. Then we found Him, and He clothed us with robes of righteousness.

Another garden, the Garden of Gethsemane, was the oil press. It was the place of crushing, of travail, where Jesus bared His soul before His Father. He prayed, "Not My will, but Thine, be done." Jesus knew He faced the road to Calvary. The stroke of the judgment of God would fall upon Him. When the cup was held out to Him in Gethsemane, He recoiled in horror, then drank it to the last drop. Figuratively speaking, in the cup swirled the stagnated sin of fallen humanity. It held every opposition to the holiness of God, past, present, and future. It included your sin and mine.

"Father, if it be possible, let this cup pass from Me," He prayed. *"Nevertheless not My will, but Thine, be done"* (Matthew 26:39; Luke 22:42).

So it is that we have our personal Gethsemane when we walk with our hand in the Savior's. When we suffer for righteousness' sake, when we are confronted with conflict, it is then that He leads us into the fellowship of His sufferings.

Then there is the garden where we find a tomb. Surely it is a garden now, for the Victor turns our graveyard experiences into gardens. Like Mary, we stoop to peer into the tomb and find it is indeed empty.

And we are no longer alone.

In the study of the tabernacle, we learn the symbolic meanings of the colors and materials that went into its construction. Thus, we associate those meanings with the description that is given of the court of the king's palace in Susa.

> *The garden had hangings of white and blue linen, fastened with cords of white linen and purple material to silver rings on marble pillars. There were couches of gold and silver on a mosaic pavement of porphyry, marble, mother-of-pearl and other costly stones.*   Esther 1:6, NIV

The tabernacle curtains were made of *"fine twined linen, and blue, and purple, and scarlet"* fastened together with clasps of gold. The boards of the tabernacle rested upon sockets of silver. Furthermore, the veil which separated the Holy Place where the priests ministered before the Lord from the Most Holy Place that the high priest entered but once a year was made of fine twined linen (see Exodus 26). Aaron, the high priest, and his sons, who ministered as priests, were dressed in designated garments of fine twined linen, and the high priest wore a breastplate containing twelve precious stones representing the twelve tribes of Israel.

> *And you shall make holy garments for Aaron your brother, for glory and for beauty.*   Exodus 28:2, NASB

The symbolism related to the tabernacle is rich with meaning, which the reader who is in unfamiliar territory would do well to explore. For our purposes we refer but briefly to the meaning represented in the text before us. Again, we turn to the book of Revelation for our interpretation of the fine linen.

Let us be glad and rejoice, and give honour to Him: for the marriage of the Lamb is come, and His wife hath made herself ready. And to her was granted that she should be arrayed in fine linen, clean and white: for the fine linen is the righteousness of saints. Revelation 19:7-8

Zechariah speaks of Zion as the apple of God's eye. *"I will be the glory in her midst"* (Zechariah 2:5, NASB).

We are clothed with the righteousness of Christ, not for our own purposes, but *for glory and for beauty*. His presence in our midst is our glory; His holiness, Our beauty.

Glory and honour are in His presence.…Worship the LORD *in the beauty of holiness.* 1 Chronicles 16:27, 29

Peter said we are being built into a spiritual house, *"an holy priesthood"* (1 Peter 2:5). We have a new identity that is represented by purple robes of royalty. As kings and priests unto God we are to walk in His authority.

If you will walk in My ways, and if you will perform My service, then you will also govern My house and also have charge of My courts. Zechariah 3:7, NASB

The Kingdom of our God is a glorious Kingdom.

We see that these hangings were fastened to silver rings and pillars of marble. The apostle Paul called the Ephesian believers *"an habitation of God through the Spirit,"* built upon *"the foundation of the apostles and prophets"* (Ephesians 2:20, 22). Silver represents redemption, and thus we see that it is through our salvation that we may stand with those pillars, the apostles, which Christ the cornerstone chose as the foundation of His Church.

His redeemed are complete in Him. As He looks at us through the blood of His Son, that is how God the Father sees us. Positionally, through the blood of the everlasting covenant, the Holy Spirit has sealed us unto the day of redemption (Ephesians 4:30).

> *And they gave them drink in vessels of gold, (the vessels being diverse one from another,) and royal wine in abundance, according to the state of the king.*   Esther 1:7

They drank from diversified vessels. Each was different, just as we are unique in our individuality.

Large goblets. Skinny goblets. Sturdy goblets. Fragile goblets. Some attractive, others ugly, but all useful.

> *Now in a large house there are not only gold and silver vessels, but also vessels of wood and of earthenware, and some to honor and some to dishonor.*
> 2 Timothy 2:20, NASB

The apostle Paul said, *"But we have this treasure in earthen vessels, that the excellency of the power may be of God, and not of us"* (2 Corinthians 4:7). He desires vessels of honor.

One mistake we may make once we have entered into a deeper walk with the Lord, is to emulate another's anointing as we observe and desire the Lord's workings in their life. We are one body but many members, and *"one and the same Spirit works..., distributing to each one individually just as He wills"* (1 Corinthians 12:11, NASB). The apostle Paul urges the individuality of the believer, yet stresses that *"to each one is given the manifestation of the Spirit for the common good"* (1 Corinthians 12:7, NASB).

Perhaps you have had the experience of listening to preaching so anointed that the minister's countenance shone with the light of God's glory. You knew it was God because the atmosphere was charged; and when you left a service like that, you recognized that something within you had been changed.

I experienced this when I attended a summer Bible conference. The room was filled with adult students chattering away, and moments before the class was scheduled to begin, the instructor softly entered the classroom. There was a holy hush, for she had brought a sense of a new presence with her. You may ask, was not the Lord with you before this? Of course He was, but into the room with this lady entered a new dimension of His presence. Awareness swept over the entire class, and we were blessed.

It was obvious that she had been with the Lord; she had been spending time waiting upon Him. Her ministry to us was effortless. She did not have to pump anything up. Every word was charged, and we recognized it. There was no fanfare. Her apparent humility was like a breath of fresh air in comparison with the circus to which we are so frequently exposed.

I left that class saying in my heart, "Lord, I want

what she's got!" And He sweetly replied, "No, you really want Me. Here I am. Come to Me."

I will never get "what she's got," for our King pours into vessels of various kinds. He may impart, bestow, communicate to me from the same storehouse from which another draws, but the supply is from Him.

And the royal wine was plentiful according to the king's bounty. And the drinking was done according to the law, there was no compulsion, for so the king had given orders to each official of his household that he should do according to the desires of each person.   Esther 1:7-8, NASB

Therein lies the secret. *Our portion will be measured out according to our desire.* The wine was there, but they were not compelled to drink. They drank according to their personal pleasure.

He does not force us to drink. Since wine is a symbol of joy, we may conclude that joy is our option. We do not have to live as those without hope for He promises to turn our sorrows into joy, even as He turned water into wine at the wedding at Cana. Our drinking is limited only by our lack of thirst, our reservations, and our self-satisfactions.

OUR DESIRE FOR HIM, AND HIM ALONE IS A GATEWAY TO HIS DIVINE DISCLOSURE.

Has our watered-down experience run out? Are the wells dry? His question comes to us as it did the sons of Zebedee, *"Are you able to drink the cup that I drink?"*

They answered, *"We are able."*

Jesus said, *"You shall indeed drink of the cup that I drink of; and with the baptism that I am baptized shall you be baptized."* (see Mark 10:35-41.)

The vessels were gold, and gold symbolizes divinity. Only His divine touch upon these earthen vessels could make them of any possible use to Him. He desires to pour Himself into us according to our thirst for Him.

Are we able to drink from His cup?

There is only one way to find out.

3

The King's Invitation

But the queen Vashti refused to come at the king's commandment.   Esther 1:12

We are willing to come to the Lord's Table for a cup of wine. But will we come just for Him? The cup was offered and we accepted it, thinking, now, finally, we have found boundless joy! Then we looked into the cup.

Looking unto Jesus the author and finisher of our faith; who for the joy that was set before Him endured the cross, despising the shame, and is set down at the right hand of the throne of God.   Hebrews 12:2

You mean the cross casts its shadows here, just when we have begun to sip the wine? His invitation is the same for each of us. Come.

Now Queen Vashti, gave a feast for the women....,

"On the seventh day, when the heart of the king was merry with wine," he commanded his seven attendants "to bring Vashti the queen before the king with the crown royal, to show the people and the princes her beauty: for she was fair to look on. But the queen ... refused to come. Esther 1:10-12

Bible commentators explain that Vashti refused to respond to the king's request because she objected to being put on display before the drunken princes of the court, which would demean her position as queen.

Nevertheless, the king had called for her.

We have a heavenly Bridegroom, a King who is sensitive to our nature. He is our Creator-Redeemer, but He will never cross the barrier of our will. His motives and purposes in our lives are pure, even when we do not understand the methods He employs to fulfill those purposes. Unlike the king who had summoned Vashti or any other human authority, we can trust our King Jesus. He will never ask us to do what is not for our good, and the highest and the best for us.

Apart from the commentator's view, when we consider Queen Vashti's refusal, there are at least three reasons why she may have responded as she did. Although these reasons are purely speculative, they may lend insight into our own spiritual deficiencies in our response to the Lord's bidding.

First, it may have been untimely. Perhaps Queen Vashti wondered why the king had sent for her at this particular time. Remember, the account mentions that Vashti was giving a feast for the women in the royal house. Surely the king would not call her now!

But Lord, there is so much to do and I'm so tired. There is a good movie on TV.

At times His nudging may seem to be unreasonable or illogical. But our King is fair. He is all knowledge. Again, He knows what is best for us, and what He has planned for our lives is far better than our greatest efforts in our own behalf. The times that He chooses to call are in His hands.

Another reason that may have been at the root of Vashti's insubordination is a lack of respect for the king. As we evaluate our own spiritual growth we find the key is obedience, a submission that is born of love.

In 1 Samuel 15:22, NASB, we read, *"To obey is better than sacrifice, and to heed than the fat of rams."*

In the Old Testament law of the offerings, the priests were instructed to take the fat that covered the inwards and the two kidneys and the fat that was upon them; and we find this interesting word: *"And the priest shall burn them upon the altar: it is the food of the offering made by fire for a sweet savor: all the fat is the LORD'S"* (Leviticus 3:16).

Now refer back to 1 Samuel: *"To obey is better…than the fat of rams."* For some reason the fat had special significance to the Lord. *All the fat is the Lord's.* Yet Samuel said that to obey is better than all of that.

There is another word in Nehemiah that sheds a bit more light on the issue. The rebuilding of the wall was finished. Nehemiah and his workers had completed the task, which the Lord had placed upon their hearts; and now, after tremendous obstacles had been overcome the job was finally done. It was a solemn yet joyous occasion as the Law was read publicly, and Nehemiah, under the unction of the Holy One of Israel, said,

"Go your way, eat the fat, and drink the sweet, and send portions unto them for whom nothing is prepared: for this day is holy unto our LORD: neither be ye sorry; for the joy of the LORD is your strength."　　　Nehemiah 8:10

The only time we can experience true joy is when we are eating the fat, when we are at the Lord's Table partaking of Him. *When we are walking in obedience, following the Holy Spirit's leading,* we indicate our respect for Him.

When the centurion came to Jesus, he said in effect, *"I am a man of authority. I know what it is to have men do what I command. I recognize that You have power and authority. You can heal my servant"* (see Matthew 8:5ff). He knew what it meant to command respect and to show it.

He respected the authority of the scepter of our King. Do we? The key is obedience.

Jesus said, *"All power is given unto Me"* (Matthew 28:18).

He also said, *"Behold, I give unto you power"* (Luke 10:19).

We try to exercise His authority to bind Satan's power when we have not yet demonstrated obedience to His authority over us in the simple things like, *"Could ye not watch with Me one hour?"* (Matthew 26:40).

This brings us to a third possible reason for the queen's response.

She may have had a waning appreciation for his favor and presence. She lost sight of all he had done for her, the many gifts he had given to her. The favor he had shown her, the authority he released into her hands, were now taken for granted. Whereas she had once delighted to be called his chosen one, to be summoned into his presence, to cater to his desires — now she had grown cold, and was caught up in her own thing. No longer did she seek only to please the king. She found her own feast more important, although all these good things had come from his hand.

But the king had power to give and power to take away.

Rather than operating as a New Testament church, in demonstration of Holy Ghost power, we try everyone else's formulas.

The latest self-help techniques. Another how-to.

We read books, watch videos, attend seminars. But when we try to make it work, nothing happens.

We have substituted everything possible for His presence, His glory.

Before we pass on from the reasons given, there is an aspect of this proposition that touches not only our relationship with the Lord, but also our interactions with one another.

It is said that familiarity breeds contempt. We can become so familiar with family and friends that we treat them shabbily. Being real does not give us license to abuse others. When we do, we bring hurt to ourselves, for we are all members of one body. We become instruments of spiritual self-abuse.

We have considered the queen's refusal, but why did the king send for Queen Vashti in the first place?

"On the seventh day [symbolic of completion, of rest] ... [the king sent for Queen Vashti] *to show the people and the princes her beauty: for she was fair to look on."*
Esther 1:10-11

The king desired to display her beauty. God is going to present "a glorious Church, not having spot, or wrinkle, or any such thing; but that it [she] *should be holy and without blemish."*
Ephesians 5:27

Our heavenly Father is preparing a Bride for His Son. Jesus has paid the penalty for sin, and He deserves to have a spotless Bride. His Bride will stand in His presence, not through any works of righteousness, but through an inward work of the Spirit.

We saw that as individual vessels, our Father views us through the Blood of His Son. As a corporate body, He sees a glorious, overcoming Church. As we are *preparing* to be His Bride, what is our King's response to our lack of response to Him?

Our King has infinite grace and mercy, but who can deny those occasions in Scripture where we see His resultant action when all else has failed? You will recall that God's people, the nation of Israel, grew cold and rebelled against God in disobedience and backslidings. Time after time they refused to heed Jehovah's warnings through the prophets. Like Queen Vashti, they refused to respond to His invitation. God's people, who had been delivered from the tyranny of the Egyptians by the mighty arm of God, would someday weep for His lost favor under Babylonian captivity.

The king became angry and called for his counselors, and asked, "What shall we do?"

Does our King become angry? In 2 Samuel 6:7, we read that Uzzah died by the ark of God. God smote him for steadying the ark upon the cart when it was being moved into Jerusalem.

David cried, "How shall the ark of God come to me?"

The ark was never to be transported on a cart. It was to be carried on poles upon the shoulders of the priests. We are called to be kings and priests unto Him, and we are to carry the presence of God to those who need Him. When we fail in our responsibility, His word comes to us as it did to the church at Laodicea: *"I know your deeds* [works]*, that you are neither cold nor hot; I would that you were cold or hot. So because you are luke-warm, and neither hot nor cold, I will spit you out of My mouth"* (Revelation 3:15, NASB). God vomits out our lukewarm condition. When we are below His highest and best for us, we sicken Him.

We are to carry His presence.

Queen Vashti refused the king's invitation. May the Holy Spirit help us to realize the implications as we personally apply this word. Vashti's refusal may represent our own flesh and the self-life, which carry the seeds of rebellion. We would rather enjoy our own feast than share in the King's! When self-interests become more important than His pleasure, we fail to come into His banqueting house where He spreads a table before us in the presence of our enemies.

We see in Revelation 4:11 that the purpose for our creation is the Lord's pleasure. *"Thou art worthy, O Lord, to receive glory and honor and power: for Thou hast cre-ated all things, and for Thy pleasure they are and were created."*

The Lord takes pleasure in us. He enjoys our company, our fellowship, and our friendship. He looks forward to our times of waiting in His presence.

OBEDIENCE—OUR IMMEDIATE RESPONSE TO HIM IS THE GATEWAY TO HIS PRESENCE.

Make it personal.

My Lord is touched when I sit at His feet. He is delighted when I strum a tune to Him on my guitar, when I worship and sing to Him my love song.

We will find that the more time we spend with Him alone, the more frequently He will invite us. The more we are with Him, the more we will want to be.

But when we refuse His invitation and ignore the nudging of the Holy Spirit to draw aside into that inner chamber with Him alone, He is grieved. *And we close the gate.*

Perhaps at those times there is a controversy in Heaven.

What is being said...?

4

Controversy in Heaven

Esther 1:13-22

The king said to the wise men, which knew the times,...
What shall we do?   Esther 1:13,15

There is a controversy in Heaven. We know this by the
life of Job, and by the controversy that Satan had with
God over him.

> *"Now there was a day when the sons of God came to present*
> *themselves before the LORD, and Satan came also among*
> *them."*   Job 1:6

The account tells that the Lord pointed to Job as an
example of a blameless and upright man who feared
God (see Job 1:8). Putting it in our setting today, Satan
retorted:

"You have put a hedge of protection about him! No
wonder he behaves! He makes a good living. He has a

nice home with a brand-new satellite dish and a swimming pool in the backyard. He lacks nothing. His children are a little on the rowdy side, but all in all, Job has a good family."

So there is controversy in Heaven between God and Satan. If we recreate the scenario and put ourselves in Job's place, what would the Lord say about our love and devotion to Him? And how would Satan answer?

It is interesting to note that Job offered burnt offerings for his children when they went off to do their own thing, to have their own feasts. The first attack of Satan's was against Job's animals. Job now had no means of offering sacrifices. Anything could happen, and it did. The hedge of protection, the blood sacrifices was gone.

In the last chapter of Job, the Lord spoke to Eliphas and told him to take seven bullocks and seven rams, "and go to my servant Job, and offer up for yourselves a burnt offering." Then we read that the Lord also accepted Job. It was after this that the Lord turned his captivity and restored all he had lost and more.

Unlike Job, we need never be caught off guard. Our Perfect Sacrifice, Jesus, has been offered up once and for all. As we point to the Cross, we wipe the smile off Satan's face and foil his plan. The controversy stops there. We have no plea but the atoning blood of the Lamb, and it is more than enough.

But I wonder about other controversies that may be taking place in the courts of Heaven, controversies between the Persons of the Godhead. Could it be that the Father, the Son, and the Holy Spirit meet in my behalf, based upon my response to the King's bidding?

What shall We do? How may We draw her to Us? Why does she not respond when We call? Who is enticing her away from Our love? Where is the love she once expressed for Us?

What is being said in the courts of Heaven where we are concerned? If we are not in a process of continual spiritual growth, we are grieving the Holy Spirit. This maturing process progresses in direct relation to our response to the Lord. When the King bids us come into His chamber and we refuse to respond, how will He react?

Our lives will emit either a fragrance or a stench. The king's counselors said, "Divorce her." Vashti's behavior would affect others. Other wives in the kingdom would follow Vashti's example and treat their husbands with contempt. Such undermining of authority could not be risked.

When we pursue our own interest in preference to the King's chambers, He has no choice but to allow us the freedom of that choice. He hates divorce, but He will not violate our will. And His heart breaks.

Paul told the Thessalonian believers, *"You became followers of us and the Lord. You were examples to all that believe in Macedonia and Achaia"* (see 1 Thessalonians 1:6-8). We do not live unto ourselves. Our example will affect others whether we intend it or not.

Jesus said, *"He who is faithful in a very little thing is faithful also in much; and he who is unrighteous in a very little thing is unrighteous also in much"* (Luke 16:10, NASB). The Lord, by His Holy Spirit, will move us from the mundane into a realm of ministry if we will exercise faithfulness in the little things.

When I was a young homemaker, I hated housework. It is not my favorite thing to this day, but the Lord taught me something about His ways. I used to hide the dirty dishes in a dishpan under the sink until every dish in the cupboard was dirty. When I became a Christian, my love for the Lord made me zealous to serve Him in any capacity. I clipped the hedges around the church, worked in the nursery, cleaned the building, and counted it a joy to do whatever I could. But deep inside, I felt His tug upon my life, and was eager to get my feet wet in ministry, perhaps by teaching a Sunday school class. One day I was washing the mountain of dishes when God spoke to my heart. He said, "If you cannot fulfill the simple, mundane responsibilities of your life, how can I entrust you with MY work, with ministry?" He prepared me for His work by teaching me to conduct my personal affairs in a more orderly fashion.

"If it please the king, let there go a royal commandment from him,…That Vashti come no more before king Ahasuerus." The saying pleased the king. They also said, *"Let the king give her royal estate unto another that is better than she"* (Esther 1:19).

Queen Vashti was like the daughters of Jerusalem in the Song of Solomon. They appreciated the king and enjoyed his favor, but their relationship with him fell short of the deeper intimacy of the bride. They were not among those who press in to minister to the king. They were caught up in other things, rather than longing after him.

He will give us what we want. The decree went out, and it went forth that Queen Vashti come no more before the king. Her last opportunity for special favor and a place of acceptance where she could minister, not to others, but to the king for his pleasure, had passed.

There were three disciples out of twelve who followed Jesus a bit closer. Peter, James, and John were with Him when the others were not. They were with Him on the mount of transfiguration. They accompanied Him to the Garden of Gethsemane. They fell asleep, it is true, but at least they were there.

And out of those three, *there was one who leaned upon His breast.*

We need to evaluate our experience with the Lord to discover where we are within those three categories. The Scriptures say that some followed Him afar off.

Lord, may this not be said of us.

The Lord is gracious. He feeds us, deals with us, and ministers to us at the level of our desire toward Him. He not only gives us what we want, but as much as we want.

Do we desire manna? Or do we prefer the fleshpots of Egypt?

After these things, when the wrath of king Ahasuerus was appeased, he remembered Vashti, and what she had done, and what was decreed against her.　　　　Esther 2:1

He felt bad. He had second thoughts. He wanted her company.

When we continually refuse to come into our King's presence, we are subject to the principle, *"My spirit will not always strive with man"* (Genesis 6:3). The Holy Spirit does not strive with unbelievers alone; He strives also to win the affections of God's children who fail to appreciate His presence, who ignore His nudging.

We are not talking about losing our salvation.

We are addressing the possibility of closing the gate to a privileged place of intimacy with the Lord.

There are always those who hang around the shore, who fail to get their feet wet. The call comes equally to each of us to *"launch out into the deep"* (Luke 5:4). We may not always be as alert as we should be, and our efforts to follow Him all the way may be pitiful even in our own eyes; but He will honor the slightest desire toward Him and enable us to overcome our personal temptations and weaknesses.

Knowing the Lord in the intimacy of the inner chamber experience will have far-reaching results. We are drawn to Him for eternal purposes. As we learn to walk in the Spirit, live in the Spirit, and abide in His love moment by moment, we will discover "hidden manna."

To him that overcometh will I give to eat of the hidden manna. Revelation 2:17

Only those who overcome may eat of this manna.

AN APPRECIATION FOR HIS PRESENCE IS THE GATEWAY TO THE HIDDEN MANNA.

"The king said to the wise men, which knew the times…" (Esther 1:13). There is a controversy.

If we want to move within the prophetic realm, we

must have an ear tuned to the times, and a quickening of the Holy Spirit to correlate the Scriptures to the times in which we live. This is a spiritual function. It cannot be learned, but it is developed as we discipline ourselves. We develop sensitivity to His voice as we spend time with Him. As we wait in His presence with the Word opencd before us, He will quicken us and disclose Himself to us. Every hour spent in His presence, even when there is little or no feeling, will impart something more of His nature into our spirits.

These times in His chamber must become increasingly valued. His presence must be desired at all costs lest we, like Samson, lose the strength of our devotion and turn to self-centered interests.

The king loved Vashti, for even after divorcing her, he remembered with longing what they had experienced together.

But she had made her choice. We too have a choice to make.

It had better be the right one....

5

Afterwards

Esther 2:1-11

After these things when the anger of King Ahasuerus had subsided, he remembered Vashti and what she had done and what had been decreed against her.

Esther 2:1, NASB

After what things? In chapter one, the king has just relieved Queen Vashti of her royal duties, and the call for a new queen has been proclaimed throughout the region.

Pause with this phrase, *after these things.*

There is always an afterwards. Our response today will largely determine our spiritual growth and development in the days to come. The Lord is grieved when we break fellowship with Him, but He is governed by our will, our power of choice; and His will only overrides ours when in His sovereignty He intervenes.

There are times when He steps in because He knows

of our deeply imbedded desire toward Him. He tries to draw us to Himself by stirring a hunger, a thirst for spiritual things, for a deeper walk with Him. He allows dissatisfaction with our present spiritual plateau, even when we are active and involved in ministry. He uses various means.

Other interventions may occur because He is moved by prayer, either our own or that of others. The importance of praying for others whom we sense are not walking as closely to the Lord as He would desire is unquestionable. His intervention is a demonstration of His mercy.

There is an afterwards, and in this case we read, "after these *things.*" After what things, at this time in our lives?

Many of our lives are occupied with "things," especially in American culture. The anthropologist would point out that man as such could be traced in his sojourn through each generation because of his "things." He takes as many things with him as he can, yet always leaves traces of his things behind. The archaeologist, too, bases his facts upon his findings, the "things" which civilizations have left behind, the buried things.

What "things" are buried in our spirits? The Holy Spirit is on a "dig" within human spirits. When His wooing no longer stirs us, He digs in an effort to uncover, to expose *to our own eyes* the rubble we have collected.

Things.

Some of us have been ignoring divine dealings for years. For many, the dealings are hardly recognized any longer. Sermons no longer set us afire with a passion that was once a flame. We have grown cold.

Part of the problem may be our lifestyle.

Our homes are filled with things, and very few of them could be classified as necessities. Then too, our time, the twenty-four-hour day allotted to each of us, gets jammed with things to do; and the value of many of our preoccupations would probably fall into the wasted time category.

What drives us to accumulate so much that we little need, and disregard the cause of Christ and the poverty around us? What makes us spend more time playing than praying? And how will our spiritual growth and our relationship with the Lord be influenced by our present lifestyle?

Each of us must answer these soul-searching questions for ourselves. But before we gloss over them we must pause at the *afterwards.*

Perhaps if we consider yet other instances of "afterwards" we may be able to get a handle on our own lack of self-discipline. This phrase is used a number of times in Scripture, and whenever it appears, we should look at the preceding context to see what happened before.

It is a matter of cause and effect.

In the gospel of John, in chapter 21, we read, *"After these things Jesus showed Himself."* After what things? Obviously, He showed Himself *after* the crucifixion; *after* He cried, "It is finished!" He showed Himself *after* He rose from the dead and came out of the tomb.

He showed Himself.

Who would deny that the Church needs a revelation of the risen Christ? Yet our *personal* response must be, I desire a fresh revelation of the risen Lord; *I want Him to show Himself to me.*

Perhaps another of our problems is unbelief. We believe the Lord is with us; we are saved, baptized in the Spirit, and on our way to Glory. But do we believe He will reveal Himself to us now? We settle for far less than He intends.

He is the revealer, the One who unveils, and the Divine Disclosure. He is not satisfied to be buried in our past. We love to talk about the power of God yesterday, but what of now? *"Jesus Christ the same yesterday, and to-day and for ever"* (Hebrews 13:8).

When we can say with Paul, "I am crucified with Christ," our Lord will show Himself to us. It was the risen Christ who showed Himself to Paul on the road to Damascus. Paul was ready. He may have been on his way to persecute the Christians, but God knew his heart, his hunger, and his dedication. He was a go-getter, and a lover of the Law, but God saw his potential in Christ.

God sees our potential. He sees unimaginable areas of ministry in our lives. He sees us completed, gifted, empowered.

Certainly there is a price, but He exacts from us only that which will be for our good. If we would only believe and act on that. There is no sacrifice that will not reap far more than we could scratch for ourselves. Knowing the power of His resurrection is a process of daily dying. A fine-tuning to the voice of the Lord is developed as we purpose in our hearts that we will please the King by living for Him today in a way that will bring no shame afterwards as it did with Vashti.

Yes, there is always an afterwards, and in the text before us we see that the king, disappointed and lonely, "remembered Vashti and what she had done."

We need to realize that our King knows us perfectly. The Scriptures say of Jesus, *"He knew what was in man,"* and there are instances where we are told, *"He knew their thoughts"*. Surely we cannot hide any lack of enthusiasm we may have toward the Lord; but on the other hand, He knows also the slightest spark of desire we may possess. Our King's love is not to be compared with any natural emotion. He will do all in His power to draw us into a more intimate relationship with Himself short of violating our will.

Sometimes it is a matter of spiritual timing.

Many years ago a missionary to India, would decide "on the spur of the moment" to come to the States, and likewise return to India. People misinterpreted him because he would suddenly be on the phone, unannounced. They felt he should have sent advance notice, but they did not understand the principle upon which he operated.

When God said, "Go," he went. No wonder he often avoided political upheavals and extreme weather conditions. *He learned to recognize the voice of the Lord and acted on it without question.*

Isn't that the kind of Christian life we long for? Imagine the excitement and adventure of it. The book of Acts is full of this kind of obedience.

If we will submit ourselves to the processes, the Lord

47

will teach us to recognize His voice. We must be willing to risk making mistakes, or to make fools of ourselves if necessary in order to learn the difference between His voice and our imagination.

The Lord may use common, seemingly insignificant events to teach us to recognize His leading and to discern spiritual timing.

An example of this can be found in the story of Rags. Rags, a cross between a golden retriever and a dachshund, belonged to my eldest son's family. They were called by the Lord to return to Bible school and were unable to find a home for Rags. So they took her to the humane society.

I already had a dog, but when I learned of this, something inside me revolted. The impression received is hard to explain. The Lord had never spoken to me in this way before. It was like an alarm or a signal, and I knew I had to get Rags. Well, I temporarily "adopted" her, and started to search for a home for her. I felt from the start that I was not to keep her, so I advertised; but there was no response. Several weeks passed and at times I wondered whether my ear had been in tune. One Sunday afternoon, weeks after placing the ad, I received a phone call.

The lady said, "Do you still have the dog?" and I replied that I did.

She said, "Before you tell me anything about her, let me tell you what happened."

She told me she had wanted a golden retriever for her son who has cerebral palsy and is confined to a wheelchair. She was washing dishes when the Lord impressed, "If you look in the paper, you will find your dog." She did not have a current paper, just the back issue in which my ad appeared. Needless to say, she got the dog. Rags "ministers" to the boy, and she is in the home designed just for her. The family is in ministry, and Rags goes along on most of their evangelistic trips.

Had I ignored the impression, I would have missed two valuable experiences (and Rags a good home): recognizing the voice of the Lord in a new way; and seeing God's hand at work in having Rags available in His appointed time.

Our experiences help us to build upon our present knowledge of the Lord's ways. Each time He speaks in a new way, we are stretching and growing, becoming more sensitive to Him. As we move according to His impetus, the timing will be right.

Esther had come to the Kingdom, a higher Kingdom than she realized, for such a time as this. The stage was set. The characters were in place. The Holy Spirit was whispering the cues. She was introduced this way:

> *"And he* [Mordecai] *brought up Hadassah, that is, Esther, his uncle's daughter: for she had neither father nor mother, and the maid was fair and beautiful; whom Mordecai, when her father and mother were dead, took for his own daughter.*
> Esther 2:7

It is said that the name Esther means, "star," a pertinent fact since our Savior's birthplace was marked by the star in the east. He is *"the root and the offspring of David, and the bright and morning star"* (Revelation 22:16).

A simple Jewish maiden, orphaned and reared by

49

her cousin, appeared on the scene, not by chance, but in God's perfect time. Mordecai had heard the decree of the king, who was on a search throughout the land for that one who would please him.

So Esther was brought to the king's house and placed with those maidens who hoped for the king's favor. Hegai, who was keeper of the women, was pleased with her. In fact, Esther was preferred, given special quarters, and provided with all that she needed for her purification.

Now trusting Mordecai, and under his instructions, Esther did not let anyone know that she was Jewish. Esther would later be used to bring salvation to her people because of Mordecai's keen sense of spiritual timing. Little did he know how sharp his senses were. He was the hub in the wheel.

We will not always know the Lord's timing. Mordecai did not know the lives of the Jews would be threatened. He was simply following the dictates of his heart. The Lord reveals His hand at His own choosing. We are to obey without knowing the outcome in advance. He gives the *signs* of His times.

We may abort God's purposes in our lives if we are not tuned in to His timetable. This is so true in seasons of praying for a sovereign move of the Lord. We expect God to move yesterday, and sometimes we despair and give up just short of His timing for a breakthrough.

Lord, it is so hard to wait.

Only as the Holy Spirit strengthens us, as we are led by the Spirit, as we walk in the Spirit, as we live in the Spirit will we reach this dimension of the inner witness.

It is a honing of our spiritual senses, developed over

time and through experience. Time with the Lord. Time to grow and develop and to experience His moving in our lives. Through trial and error, our trust in His ways is developed. We find that He is faithful to us even when we are not faithful.

It is a day-to-day process.

We may make the mistake of trying to spiritualize everything when God's intention is to translate our spiritual insights into our physical circumstances. When we consider the lives of saints who led Spirit-filled lives, those who lived on a higher plane spiritually than the average churchgoer, we may get the impression that they were spiritual giants. We feel we will never attain their level of spirituality. We read books like *Praying Hyde*, and despair. Not many of us are in a position financially to be able to spend days on our knees.

So we give up. We think the deeper life experience is not for us. Many of us plod doggedly just to exist, to earn a living. Then there are a million other demands upon us, legitimate family concerns.

We feel like we are in a rat race, and the rats win.

Not so. *The Lord is waiting to meet us right where we are.* So we are not in a position to stay on our faces before Him for an eight-hour period or even for an hour. He knows our circumstances. Some situations we have created for ourselves and they need adjustments. The big issue is whether or not He has full possession of all we are now.

Does He have priority, and do we respond to Him when He does call? If we awaken at night and find we cannot go back to sleep, do we recognize Him in it? *He may be calling.* We fret because we "need our rest" for work tomorrow. If we arise and meet with Him, He will increase our strength to exceed that of a full night's sleep.

Again, it is a matter of trust. Whose way is better?

The Lord graciously helps us make the changes that need to be made in us so He may fill every crevice, but first we must allow the principle of the Cross to work in our lives. Death to self. As repentance opens our spirits, desire for Him replaces the love of self. As we learn to respond to Him in obedience, we develop a sense of appreciation for His presence. He begins to occupy every area of our lives. As we cooperate with Him, He develops our spiritual ears.

Entering the deeper walk with the Lord is not a cloister experience. God created and loves real people. We have no conception of how much He loves us and desires communion with us. He wants to laugh with us, cry with us, walk and talk with us at every level of our lives. And as He enters our experiences and enjoys us, He will reciprocate and lead us to the realms where He dwells. He is preparing us.

TRUSTING THAT HIS WAY IS BETTER THAN OURS IS THE GATEWAY TO RECOGNIZING HIS VOICE

Esther was about to be prepared for higher purposes, but in the meantime there was a purification process through which she must pass.

And Mordecai walked every day before the court of the women's house, to know how Esther did, and what should become of her. Esther 2:11

Mordecai, the cousin of Esther and most likely quite a bit older than she, seemed to have insight into the stress imposed upon the women in the king's house. He knew the processing to which she must submit in order to be appreciated by the king. He was in tune with what was going on in Esther's life.

If we were "tuned in" to the Lord, we would know what He was doing in the lives of our loved ones. We would pray more intelligently, and thereby usher them into His purposes through our prayers.

Just as Mordecai kept in touch with Esther's preparation, the Holy Spirit watches over us with a jealous love. He has an investment in us. He will not stand by and allow us to waste the life He has breathed into us. He has imparted gifts and callings, and intends to lead us into His fullness. As our desire for purity is expressed, He will escort us through our particular processing.

It is a time of bitter-sweetness.

6

Purification

Esther 2:12-15

And the maiden pleased him [Hegai], and she obtained kindness of him; and he speedily gave her her things for purification.   Esther 2:9

It appears that every maiden, under the supervision of Hegai, had to pass a year before she was brought before the king. These were called her days of purification, *"six months with oil of myrrh, and six months with sweet odors, and with other things for the purifying of the women"* (Esther 2:12).

Interestingly, the Hebrew words used here, in respect to the purification, mean, "to rub, to polish," and signifiy purification and adornment with all kinds of precious ointments. Although we are not given the names of the spices used in this custom, the meaning of the purification becomes clear as we consider "the oil of myrrh."

In Exodus 30:22-25, we find the instructions for making the anointing oil that was used when the tabernacle was consecrated, and especially as it related to the altar of incense.

> *Moreover, the LORD spoke to Moses, saying, "Take also for yourself the finest of spices: of flowing myrrh five hundred shekels. And you shall make of these a holy anointing oil, a perfume mixture, the work of a perfumer; it shall be a holy anointing oil."* NASB

Moses was instructed to anoint the tent of meeting, all of its furniture and utensils, and finally Aaron and his sons. In the study of typology we learn that Aaron the high priest represents Christ, and Aaron's sons represent the Church. From this we conclude that the Church, the Body of Christ, is to be anointed with the oil of the Holy Spirit. Note verse 31: *"This shall be a holy anointing oil to Me throughout your generations."*

We will not deal with all the spices used in this holy anointing oil because our text in Esther is concerned only with "the oil of myrrh." In order to consider the oil of myrrh, we will look at several other scriptures.

Psalm 45 is referred to as *A Song of Celebration for the King's Marriage.* How appropriate is verse eight: *"All Thy garments are fragrant with myrrh and aloes and cassia"* (NASB). This psalm was the inspiration for the lovely hymn "Ivory Palaces", which speaks of the incarnation of our King Jesus, who left the glories of Heaven to enter a "world of woe."

His garments were fragrant with myrrh.

To broaden our understanding we turn our attention to the Song of Solomon, another picture of the relationship between the one being prepared as bride and her bridegroom.

"A bundle of myrrh is my well-beloved unto me" (Song of Solomon 1:13). *Our beloved is Christ, the Messiah, the Anointed One.* Again, in Song of Solomon 4:6 (NASB): *"Until the cool of the day when the shadows flee away, I will go my way to the mountain of myrrh and to the hill of frankincense."*

What a beautiful prophetic word concerning Calvary! Jesus went to Calvary in the sweetness of the anointing, not in the bitterness of gall. This is hard to understand, for it is contrary to our nature. But Jesus moved in the anointing of the Holy Spirit.

One more word is found in the Song of Solomon 5:5: *"I rose up to open to my beloved; and my hands dropped with myrrh, and my fingers with sweet smelling myrrh, upon the handles of the lock."*

Where King Jesus has been, there lingers a sweet fragrance, an anointing.

It is no longer a mystery that among the gifts brought to the newborn King were gold and frankincense and myrrh (see Matthew 2:11). Certainly these were symbolic of His life and death. In the closing moments of His life on earth before the resurrection, we find reference to the myrrh.

> *And they tried to give Him wine mixed with myrrh; but He did not take it.*   Mark 15:23, NASB

He had already drunk the cup of bitterness at Gethsemane; He had totally ingested it into His being.

57

It could not be sweetened from the hand of man. His perfect union with His Father sweetened it. *"I delight to do Thy will, O my God: yea, Thy law is within My heart"* (Psalm 40:8).

Finally, we find that after the crucifixion, Joseph of Arimathea and Nicodemus brought spices containing a mixture of myrrh and aloes, and wrapped our Lord's body with the spices, again a prophetic picture of His bittersweet death (see John 19:38-40).

Even as Esther was anointed with oils for her purification, the Church is preparing for that moment when she will be ushered into the presence of the King of kings and Lord of lords. *She is being purified.* The King has provided all she needs for her purification. It is His purpose to come for a Church without blemish.

Personal Purity is the Gateway to Power

In order to accomplish this, He is dealing with individual lives within the Church. He is dealing with us. *He is doing a work of purification.* He is rubbing, and polishing, and putting us through the testings of fire to burn out all that is offensive to Him.

At times we hinder His work. Although we are tested, tried, and proved, we should not allow spiritual blockages in our lives. We need not be subject to backslidings and disobedience. He has provided the anointing oil of the Holy Spirit to sweeten any bitter waters through which we may pass.

It is imperative for us to press in to the Lord and to seek His anointing. Then we will find that bondages in our lives are being broken. *"And it shall come to pass in that day, that his burden shall be taken away from off thy shoulder, and his yoke from off thy neck, and the yoke shall be destroyed because of the anointing"* (Isaiah 10:27).

In 1 John 2:27, we are assured that we have an anointing, which abides in us and will teach us. But we must be willing and obedient. We must cooperate with the purification process that the Lord desires to accomplish in our lives.

Many give their hearts to the Lord in a simple act of acceptance; but few give their lives, their beings, their all. The Lord longs for each of us to enter fully into His provision, not only for salvation but also for power to live an overcoming life.

When we draw upon spiritual resources, we have all we require.

> *Then thus came every maiden unto the king; whatsoever she desired was given her to go with her out of the house of the women unto the king's house. In the evening she went, and on the morrow she returned into the second house of the women...: she came in unto the king no more, except the king delighted in her, and that she were called by name.*
>
> Esther 2:13-14

Esther had been through the purification process in preparation to enter the king's chamber. The oil of myrrh and fragrant ointments had been administered —a preparation that lasted twelve months.

Some preparations take longer than others, but in our walk with the Lord, we find that the purifying process administered by the Holy Spirit is an ongoing one. We have lessons to learn that are only grasped as we submit to His nudging.

Malachi 3:2-3 describes the Lord as *"like a refiner's fire, and like fullers' soap: and He shall sit as a refiner and purifier of silver: and He shall purify the sons of Levi, and purge them as gold and silver, that they may offer unto the* LORD *an offering in righteousness."*

Our God knows how to extract gold from our lives. He knows how to refine our characters. He may have to apply pressure and squeeze a little here or there, but He is more interested in purifying us than in making life easy. He knows what it will take to conform us to the image of His Son, and that is His ultimate goal.

We do not always cooperate with Him. We were born children of disobedience. In the new birth, which is the foundation of our Christian experience, we are subject to a new set of spiritual genes working within our spirits. Creative processes, now developing us from the inside out, thrust us experientially into the new creation we have become.

Because we do not always cooperate, or we are perhaps spiritually dull, God provides us with space. These are transition periods in our lives, that He may accomplish in us His perfect will.

In Esther 2:14, we read, *"In the evening she went, and on the morrow she returned."* Do you realize what transpired in that period? Esther had been ushered into the king's chamber, and her whole life was changed overnight. A transition occurred. How did it happen?

First, she was ready. She had humbled herself, had submitted to the process of the ointments, the anointing. Jesus said about the woman who broke the alabaster box and poured the ointment upon Him, *"She hath wrought a good work."* He said that wherever the Gospel was preached throughout the whole world, her act of worship (for that is what it was) would be spoken of, for a memorial of her (see Mark 14:3-9). Like Esther, she humbled herself and gave the best she had to her Lord.

Next, Esther gave up her right to her own life. That was understood when she left the home of Mordecai. The psalmist prayed, *"When my father and my mother forsake me, then the LORD will take me up"* (Psalm 27:10). Jesus said, *"Whosoever will come after Me, let him deny himself, and take up his cross, and follow Me"* (Mark 8:34). Again, *"And every one that hath forsaken houses, or brethren, or sisters, or father, or mother, or wife, or children, or lands, for My name's sake, shall receive an hundredfold, and shall inherit everlasting life"* (Matthew 19:29).

Perhaps you find this concept hard to accept. But God has ways of dealing with us as individuals, and of bringing us to a place of glad surrender to Him. These are places of transition.

In the evening she went, and on the morrow she returned.

Our evenings, the darkened places of our experience, are God's opportunities to set in motion the creative forces that will bring us into His light. We must realize that even adversity and afflictions are instruments of change in our lives. In Isaiah, 30, through the lips of the prophet, God tells us that we will see our teachers. These are the bread of adversity (trouble) and the water of affliction. But we don't want to be taught by life experiences that hurt. Jesus learned obedience by the things that He suffered. Are we greater than our Lord? We wait for God to deliver us from trouble when in reality He is waiting for us to respond appropriately to the times of testing that may come. He waits to be gracious to us.

> *And therefore will the LORD wait, that he may be gracious unto you, and therefore will he be exalted, that he may have mercy upon you: for the LORD is a God of judgment: blessed are all they that wait for Him. For the people shall dwell in Zion at Jerusalem: thou shalt weep no more: He will be very gracious unto thee at the voice of thy cry; when He shall hear it, He will answer thee. And though the Lord give you the bread of adversity, and the water of affliction, yet shall not thy teachers be removed into a corner* [hidden] *any more, but thine eyes shall see thy teachers: and thine ears shall hear a word behind thee, saying, This is the way, walk ye in it, when ye turn to the right hand, and when ye turn to the left.* Isaiah 30:18-21

When we view our problems from God's perspective, we come to realize that the character changes that are necessary in order to conform us to the image of Christ are actually being wrought by His creative process within.

In the book of Genesis, every creative act was on this wise: *"And the earth was without form, and void; and darkness was upon the face of the deep. And the Spirit of God moved upon the face of the waters. And God said, Let there be light: and there was light"* (Genesis 1:2-3).

As we continue on through the passage we see that

there is a period of transition between the creation of light (day) and darkness (night), in verse four. In verse five we find the same words that we find in Esther: *"And the evening and the morning were the first day."*

Every creative act thereafter was likewise: *"Let there be.... and it was so". "And the evening and the morning were the second day."* And so on.

Our twilight times should precede the entrance of His light and of His creative processes in us. But we do have a responsibility: *In the evening she went....*

We will return on the morrow in the power of the Spirit to the measure that we allow His leading. Each time we interrupt the process, He begins again. Thankfully, we are His workmanship.

When we feed upon His Word, we are submitting to the process; when we pour out our hearts in prayer, we are allowing expression to the process. These are evening places. His desire is toward us, and as we go to Him, even experimentally, He delights in us. Before long, we will hear Him calling us by name.

No need to wait our turn now. We have found favor with Him. He bids us come.

His Word is creative. There is a door that is held ajar. The new birth is that door, opened that we may glimpse Him, but He wants us to come so that He may open the door further and further, as He discloses Himself, reveals Himself until we are drawn into His chamber where we may be changed.

In these periods we know His Word is working within us. *"The word of God is quick, and powerful, and sharper than any two-edged sword, piercing even to the dividing asunder of soul and spirit, and of the joints and marrow, and is a discerner of the thoughts and intents of the heart"* (Hebrews 4:12).

Today may be a time of transition for some. The falling shadows may be causing darkness rather than the expected light. The Lord does have light. He wants to reveal Himself to us in a new way. We dare not allow the darkness to keep us from Him, but rather it should drive us to Him; and as it does, the dayspring will arise in our hearts and we will see more clearly.

> *Now when the turn of Esther, the daughter of Abihail the uncle of Mordecai, who had taken her for his daughter, was come to go in unto the king, she required nothing. ... And Esther obtained favor in the sight of all them that looked upon her.*   Esther 2:15

This is tremendous! Esther was an orphan, and a Jewess. Normally, she would not have received preference. *She required nothing.* She asked for nothing. She was not greedy, and she did not take advantage of this unique situation in which she found herself. Yet all the other maidens were impressed with her. She possessed a beauty which was born of modesty and humility.

The Lord guides us into times of soul-searching. What is required of us to maintain purity before Him? Are we examples of Christian grace, modesty, and humility in the immoral culture within which we live? Do we hold the standard of the Word of God high within our own lives? Have the purifying fires of God so purged our lives that compromise in matters of dress and modesty has no grip upon us? Or have we been beguiled into reasoning away our convictions, measuring ourselves with others rather than by God's Word?

These are personal matters to be weighed before the Lord. In a day when morals are defiled, the Lord promises to keep that one who desires to be pure for Him.

Sexual purity *is* possible. Deliverance from drugs and alcohol *is* a reality. And saying no to sin *is* required. He provides the anointing, which sweetens, and the grace to enable. We need only submit ourselves to Him.

As we do, His rule and authority become real in our experience.

We have entered a gateway to victory....

7

The King's Gate

Esther 2:16-23

In those days, while Mordecai sat in the king's gate....
Esther 2:21

Esther's prescribed period of purification for her ap-
pearance before the king was accomplished. Now, we
are given the method by which the candidates were
presented for this special audience with the king. King
Ahasuerus sought that one who would occupy the
throne as queen.

It was customary for the virgin to go to the king's
quarters in the evening, and return on the morrow.

Stop and consider how Esther must have felt. For
twelve months, she had prepared for this moment. Separated from the only home she knew, under Mordecai's
roof, this simple, humble Jewess would now be tested.
She was to go before the king on her own.

Did her heart beat with anxiety or even fear? Or was she confident, trusting fully that her preparation was complete? Did she doubt her ability, or underestimate her own beauty? Although many coveted this honor, it must have been scary nonetheless.

A missionary shared that over twenty years ago, he had visited a foreign country other than his field of service, and while there he received an invitation for an audience with the queen. He described his reactions this way:

"I waited in the outside court with trepidation. My hands were clammy and I found myself trembling with nervousness. I had worked for years among simple village people. What would I say to this highly revered imperial? How should I conduct myself?"

Finally, his big moment arrived, and he was ushered into the presence of the queen. She was seated in an elegant but small parlor with just two chairs and a hand-carved coffee table placed in the center of the room. On the table lay an open Bible.

After the initial greetings, she invited the missionary to be seated and said, "I will share my heart with you"; then, pointing to the Bible, she added "and you will give me a word from the Lord."

The missionary described the peace that descended upon him. He was on familiar territory now. His audience with the queen was on mutual ground because they were both subjects of the same Kingdom—that of Jesus Christ, the King of kings.

And the king loved Esther above all the women, and she obtained grace and favor in his sight more than all the virgins; so that he set the royal crown upon her head, and made her queen instead of Vashti.   Esther 2:17

He was pleased with her. *She required nothing.*

We, too, have an invitation into the King's chambers—the King Himself is the Door, and He waits for an audience with us. The purification rites are perfect and complete through His precious atoning blood and the anointing of the Holy Spirit. Unlike Esther, we are not on our own as we present ourselves before our King. Ushered through the veil by His Holy Spirit, we offer His own blood. *We require nothing more.*

And He waits. Will we be a Vashti or an Esther to our King?

Time passed. To summarize, Esther the Jewess had been crowned queen, but in spite of her seat of authority, she maintained a close relationship with Mordecai, probably the only family she knew.

Mordecai was apparently one of the doorkeepers or attendants at the gate to the palace. He occupied a unique position indeed. It was there, at the king's gate, that Mordecai learned of a conspiracy against the king. He reported the matter to Esther, who in turn advised the king. When the matter was investigated, the report was found to be accurate and the culprits were hanged.

Mordecai sat in the king's gate....

In 1 Chronicles, 15, we have the account of David preparing a place for the ark of the covenant. It was to be moved to the city of David. David reminded the priests and the Levites that when the ark had previously been moved, they had separated themselves from the presence of God because they had not moved the ark according to the word of the Lord. We mentioned earlier, they had placed the ark upon a cart; but Moses had commanded, according to the word of the Lord, that the children of the Levites were to *bear the ark of God upon their shoulders.*

David had learned his lesson, and now, careful preparations were made for moving the ark. In the account there is a listing of the appointments, which were given to the Levites. There were the singers and the musicians, and *the doorkeepers for the ark.* Remember, the ark of the covenant symbolizes the presence of God.

When I meditate upon this passage, I cannot help but feel an urgency to carefully guard and revere the Lord's presence. I wonder whether we have an adequate sense of appreciation for Him. Do we value His presence in our lives, in our families, and in our churches, so much so that we are willing to watch and to wait for Him?

We realize He is with us always, but are we looking for those special times when He makes Himself real to us, when He quickens His Word to our hearts and guides us into deeper truths?

Are we sitting in the King's gate?

Now we do need to be aware that there are those at the King's gate who are not about His business.

A pastor told of a woman who came to him disturbed by the lack of commitment of several of the members of the church. Apparently, she thought they should be either in or out. This pastor gave her a lesson that Jesus taught about the Kingdom of Heaven in Matthew, 13.

A man sowed good seed in his field, but the enemy came and sowed weeds among the wheat. When the wheat grew, the weeds sprang up also. The workers wanted to pull out the weeds, but the landowner stopped them with these words:

> *"No; lest while you are gathering up the tares, you may root up the wheat with them. Allow both to grow together until the harvest; and in the time of the harvest I will say to the reapers, 'First gather up the tares and bind them in bundles to burn them up; but gather the wheat into my barn'"*
>
> Matthew 13:29-30, NASB

In the same chapter of Matthew, Jesus likens the Kingdom of Heaven to a net which was cast into the waters and gathered fish of every kind; and when it was filled, they kept the good fish, but threw away the bad (see verses 47-49).

Do not take it for granted that everyone who enters the doors of your church experiences the presence of God. Some may be wheat and some tares, but only the Lord is qualified to do the sorting. We are to let them grow together until the time of the harvest.

There are those precious moments that we spend within the inner chamber with the King, and as we experience those moments, our hearts long for more of them. But we are also given responsibilities in the King's court. These are the vineyard experiences.

In Matthew, 20, Jesus gave the parable of the man who went out early in the morning to hire laborers for his vineyard. He went out hour after hour, hiring still more laborers; and in each instance he asked, *"Why are you standing here all the day idle?"*

This tells us clearly that those moments, those hours,

those seasons which are not spent within the inner chamber ministering before the Lord are to be spent ministering to others. First Him, then others.

But our ministry to others will be empty unless we are first shut in with Him.

After that time with Him, however, we are to be about our King's business. God is still trying to move lazy Christians into His vineyard. His work should be our joy, our pleasure. Jesus said, *"My meat is to do the will of Him that sent Me, and to finish His work"* (John 4:34). No wonder David cried in Psalm 84, *"How amiable are thy tabernacles, O LORD of hosts! My soul longeth, yea, even fainteth for the courts of the LORD: my heart and my flesh crieth out for the living God."* And again, in this same psalm, *"For a day in thy courts is better than a thousand. I had rather be a doorkeeper in the house of my God, than to dwell in the tents of wickedness."*

Do we value the presence of God more than life itself? What are some of the choices we make? Do we covet the teaching of biblical principles for our children above Sesame Street? Are we able to tear ourselves away from the Super Bowl when it is time to leave for church? Are we anxious to worship, to praise our Redeemer's name, or do we use the worship part of the service to file our nails, balance our checkbook, or repair our makeup? Do we bother attending at all?

Our greatest need may be a deeper commitment to Him.

COMMITMENT IS THE GATEWAY TO SERVICE.

When He speaks a truth to us, deals lovingly with

us, and enlightens our understanding, do we guard that area of our lives reverently, prayerfully, lest it should slip from us?

Mordecai sat in the king's gate.

When you leave the inner chamber, linger at the door, serve in His courts, and value the treasures He has shown you. Impart them. They are of infinite worth.

Guard each gateway He opens to you, lest a thief break through and steal....

8

A Death Sentence

Esther 3

Let it be written that they may be destroyed. Esther 3:9

Again we read, "After these things...," so we understand that the events before us occurred after the attempted conspiracy against the king. It had failed due
to Mordecai's role as an informant. The guilty parties
had been hanged.

Now, *after these things,* the king promoted a man by
the name of Haman to a position of authority. The king
had given commandment that all the king's servants
were to bow and reverence Haman, but Mordecai
would not comply. He was a Jew. Jehovah was his God.
He could not bow to mortal man.

Mordecai's situation was similar to that of the three
Hebrew children who refused to bow to the golden
image as decreed by the king, Nebuchadnezzar. You

may recall also how Daniel's prayers were heard from the windows of his chamber, in spite of the king's decree that only the king should be worshiped.

So the situation is not unique. Mordecai found himself the object of jealousy and hatred; but in this instance there was one difference. Haman purposed to destroy, not Mordecai alone, but all the Jews throughout the whole kingdom.

Haman devised a plot which, if successful, would result in the abolishment of all the Jews. His appeal to the king was subtle and deceptive, and it was agreed that all Jews, both young and old, little children and women, would be killed.

Now that we have briefly summarized the events, refer back to these words in the first verse of the chapter: "[the king promoted Haman] and set his seat above all the princes that were with him."

Notice that the King James text uses the word *prince* to describe this wicked man's position. This word is used frequently in Scripture, especially in the Old Testament. According to the International Standard Bible Encyclopedia, the word is never used to denote royal parentage, yet often indicates actual royal or ruling power, together with royal dignity and authority. As a rule, the name is given to human beings; in a few instances it is applied to God and Christ, the angels and the devil (Vol. IV, p. 2453).

There is no doubt that the evil plot which took shape in the heart of Haman, his bribery, his murderous intent against the Jews, God's people, was diabolical. Thus, we see the satanic influence upon him.

In Ephesians 2:2, Paul speaks of the *"prince of the*

power of the air," as the spirit that now works in the children of disobedience that we once were. In John 12:31, Jesus referred to Satan as *"the prince of this world."*

We know that Satan rules in the hearts of murderers and terrorists, but we need to be alerted that, just as surely as we experience a personal God, there is a personal devil whose purpose is to discourage and confuse us to the point of spiritual death. Yes, just as surely as Satan put it in the heart of Mordecai's enemy to destroy a race of people, Satan desires today to destroy every born-again child of God. He is subtle, and in order to deceive us, he may even appear as an angel of light (see 2 Corinthians 11:14).

Scores of young people are enticed and drawn into lives of sin, experimenting with drugs, alcohol, and permissive sex. Sadly, the Church, by and large, falls into Satan's trap by compromising holy, godly standards. As the cartoon so aptly depicts, we prohibit Bible reading in our schools and approve the distribution of condoms.

The prince of the power of the air *is* coming down; but, thank God, his time is short. Jesus tells us in John 16:11 that he is already judged. Jesus Christ is the only Man who ever lived who could make the tremendous statement found in John 14:30, NIV, *"He* [the prince of this world] *has no hold on Me."*

Jesus revealed a principle of truth in this statement that will change our lives, if we grasp it. It will enable us to live in total victory. It will inject within us the courage to resist the devil, and the power to stand for righteous living in word *and* action. It will strengthen the hands of weaker, feebler Christians, and challenge them to faithfulness to their Lord as they witness the loyal-hearted devotion of God's army,

The principle is really quite simple. *To the degree that we grasp and cleave to our Lord Jesus, every hold on us must loosen.*

There is the story of a man who was fishing from a boat when a storm blew up. He attempted to row to shore, but crashed into a huge boulder. Water gushed into the boat, so the man crawled out and tried to climb onto the huge rock, but it was too smooth to grasp. In desperation, he grasped a root that was growing out of a crevice of the rock. He clung to it hour after hour, all night long. The next morning, rescuers finally found him, still clinging. When they tried to free his clasp, they discovered that the water smashing against him had dashed his hand into the crevice of the rock. He no longer held onto the rock; *the rock held him.*

Isn't it that way with us? If we start out by clinging to Him, we will find our hold upon every other thing loosening until we realize that He holds us fast.

We have a Rock upon which to stand, even Jesus. The Psalmist cried, *"Come, let us sing for joy to the LORD; let us shout aloud to the Rock of our salvation"* (Psalm 95:1, NIV).

Peter wrote that to those who stumble at His Word, He is a "rock of offense" (1 Peter 2:8). But those who love Him, and have fully consecrated their lives to Him at any cost, find in Him a shelter from the storm, the fulfillment of Isaiah's prophecy: *"Behold, a king shall reign in righteousness... And a man shall be as an hiding place from the wind, and a covert from the tempest; as rivers of water in a dry place, as the shadow of a great rock in a weary land"* (Isaiah 32:1-2).

The stormy places in our experiences as well as the bleak, barren, dry times will become gateways to refreshing waters that quench our spiritual thirst. Paul described the Israelites who wandered through the desert: *"For they drank of that spiritual Rock that followed them: and that Rock was Christ"* (1 Corinthians 10:4).

May the cry of our hearts join the psalmist's: *"Lead me to the rock that is higher than I"* (Psalm 61:2). *He will hold us fast.*

There is a certain people scattered abroad and dispersed among the people in all the provinces of thy kingdom; and their laws are diverse from all people.   Esther 3:8

God's people, His born-again children of the Kingdom, are scattered throughout the whole earth today. They constitute a great army. Their laws are different from those of any other people, and they should be, because they live, and move, and have their being in a spiritual law of love. They are the people of the Lord, a royal priesthood, a company of believers who follow a crucified, risen Christ. They are the Church triumphant.

"But you are a chosen people, a royal priesthood, a holy nation, a people belonging to God, that you may declare the praises of Him who called you out of darkness into His wonderful light.   1 Peter 2:9, NIV

The King James Version reads, *a peculiar people.* In other words, we are special.

Titus 2:14 tells us that our Savior *"gave Himself for us, that He might redeem us from all iniquity, and purify unto Himself a peculiar people, zealous of good works."*

In the Old Testament, Jehovah refers to His people as a "treasured possession" (Exodus 19:5, NIV, and other references).

Although we must adhere to the law of the land, let us never forget that our first allegiance is to God's law and His rule. We are created for His pleasure. We serve a righteous King. He does not pass laws in ignorance, nor does He toy with our emotions.

Read the law that was passed: *"To destroy, to kill, and to cause to perish,* all Jews, both young and old, little children and women, in one day..." (Esther 3:13). Does this sound familiar? Compare it with John 10:10, NASB, as Jesus describes the work of Satan: "The thief comes only *to steal, and kill, and destroy."*

All the Jews were to be killed! Notice also in verse 12 that the edict was written by the scribes in the name of the king and sealed with the king's ring. This law was devised in the heart of Haman, the enemy of God's people, yet *it was presented as from the king.*

There are times when our enemy, Satan, pronounces our doom and fools us into believing that the verdict and sentence have come from the hand of God Himself. He has convinced Christians that God sent their sicknesses. In some cases, he fools us into losing the healings we do receive.

Do you ever hear statements like these? *"God is punishing me." "This sickness must be from God." "Well, if it's God's will, I'll get better."*

We have a "sure word of prophecy" to stand upon: "With His stripes we are healed" (Isaiah 53:5; see also 1 Peter 2:24).

God desires blessing and victory for His children; but Satan on the other hand proposes our ruin. Jesus told Peter that Satan desired to have him, to sift him as wheat. But we have recourse; we are not defenseless. Jesus added, *"But I have prayed for you, that your faith may not fail; and you, when once you have turned again, strengthen your brothers"* (Luke 22:32, NASB).

Behind the scenes we, as God's people, have One who is working in our behalf, even as He was working in behalf of those Jews whom Haman was determined to kill, and to do it by the hand of the king! Even the most needy, the weakest, most frail child of God is the object of God's desire to deliver, and to move through gates of growth and maturity. It was true of Peter, and it is true of us. We are His treasured possession.

Like Aaron's rod that budded, the dead root of our sinful life may sprout and bloom with resurrection life. We do not have to accept the devil's lies about our lives and our situations. They are not hopeless. God will intervene if we let Him. His Name is above any other name, and He has given us the right and authority to its use.

A SPIRIT-DISCIPLINED THOUGHT-LIFE IS THE GATEWAY TO AUTHORITY.

Spurred on by the king's command, the couriers went out, and the edict was issued in the citadel of Susa.
                                        Esther 3:15, NIV

The command meant death.

The protagonist was an enemy.

It was intended for evil.

But God...

Not everything that transpires in our lives, even after we begin our Christian walk, is good. Sometimes we can point directly to the wicked devices of the devil and we know we are under attack. At other times the attack is subtler.

"And the edict was issued in the citadel of Susa."

A citadel is a fortress, a stronghold. Satan strives to set up fortresses in our minds that oppose the purposes of God. He thrusts impressions and ideas into our thoughts. He is trying to set up strongholds in the minds, in the thoughts of Christians today, and his thoughts will destroy us if we nurture them.

Our thoughts influence our words and our actions, and certainly our spiritual growth is largely dependent upon what we do with those thoughts that are not of God. Thus, the thought-life is a battleground.

Most of our failures and backslidings begin here. The Christian who learns to discipline his thought-life is a Christian who lives in victory, and is one who grows spiritually. An undisciplined thought-life produces spiritual retardation or worse.

Christians sometimes get confused as to which thoughts are of God and which are not. We have a sound measure, a guide, which is the Word of God. Then too, the anointing will teach us. Sometimes we may feel uncomfortable about something we hear or read, but we are not sure why. These are caution lights, not to be ignored.

The edict of your spiritual death is issued in the citadel of your thought-life. That is the fortress.

Jesus wants to be enthroned in our thought-life. He wants our will to be a fortress, a citadel against every satanic attack that would draw us from Him. Paul gives us a good prescription in Philippians 4:8, NIV: *"Finally, brothers, whatever is true, whatever is noble, whatever is right, whatever is pure, whatever is lovely, whatever is admirable – if anything is excellent or praiseworthy – think about such things."*

One of the hardest areas to control is the direction of the thought-life. We must cooperate with the Holy Spirit by resisting wrong thoughts and insisting upon healthy ones. Many emotionally disturbed people have been completely delivered by concentrating upon this area.

Those who live overcoming lives learn to *let* the mind of Christ function in them (see Philippians 2:5).

Paul not only offers a prescription, but gives the method for using it:

"For though we live in the world, we do not wage war as the world does. The weapons we fight with are not the weapons of the world. On the contrary, they have divine power to demolish strongholds. We demolish arguments and every pretension that sets itself up against the knowledge of God, and we take captive every thought to make it obedient to Christ."   2 Corinthians 10:3-5 NIV

The best way to think the thoughts of God is to read and obey His Word, even when it seems threatening. When we are obedient, when we do things His way, as His Word instructs, the results will be right—even though it does not seem logical at the time or it goes against our grain.

The Jews did not think they would live. They had received a death sentence. Although their proposed destruction was an evil design, when we continue on in the book of Esther we find that the death sentence is eventually overturned—but not without divine dealings. The reason that God *allows* (not initiates) bad things to happen to His people is for their good. Have you ever noticed that miracles seem to happen so easily for the unsaved? Or how new Christians get their prayers answered so readily? At times God uses the miracle, the deliverance, and the answered prayer to get our attention.

Miracles are no problem for God. He can give us our miracle with a snap of His fingers. If we have a problem, He can solve it. If we battle an addiction to some habit, He can deliver. He does not want us bogged down with sin, but there are problems of the flesh, our personalities, and our hang-ups that need dealing with. Through these He seeks to teach us, to train us, and in the process to change us. He could remove the problem, and chances are we would remain the same. But that does not interest Him. He wants a new me. He wants the character of His beloved Son to be formed in us, and to grow in us, and to characterize our thought-life and our subsequent actions.

It is not always deliberate disobedience or rebellion that prevents change or spiritual growth. Many times we really do not see ourselves as others do. We may readily recognize the shortcomings of our brothers and sisters, yet to our own we are blind. When we *are* led to recognize our faults, however, we are not to be impatient with others.

When the answers to prayers for change in a situation seem delayed, we need to sincerely ask the Lord to point out the changes that He is trying to make in us. The closer we are to Him, the lesser, seemingly insignificant areas in our lives will loom before us as intolerable sins.

Notice that the couriers were "spurred on" by the king's command. If we were as quick to obey the Word of the Lord to our hearts, as Satan's couriers are to do his bidding, we would mature and enter undreamed-of spiritual realms. There are strongholds, spiritual strongholds to be broken down; and we have been given the armament with which to accomplish the task. We, too, can reverse Satan's purposes in our lives.

"The city of Susa was bewildered." The city of Susa represented the Jews and the Persians both and they were confused. We get bewildered when we try to mix the spiritual with the carnal. We no longer can determine which is right. Our minds become filled with the reasonings of the world around us, and before long we are bewildered. We may even find ourselves giving in to devilish desires.

Some Christians no longer know for sure what they believe or what stands are right. We need to get back into our Bibles. In some cases, if the time spent watching TV was swapped with the devotional time, the Church would be revolutionized. We need to be saturated with the anointed, creative Word.

Remember, just as our mind can become a battlefield for Satan's evil thrusts, so our will, our mind, our thought-life may become a citadel, a fortress for the Spirit of God to set up a garrison against the enemy's attack.

The attack may be at hand....

9

Life-and-Death Intercession

Esther 4

When Mordecai perceived all that was done, Mordecai rent his clothes, and put on sackcloth with ashes, and went out into the midst of the city, and cried with a loud and a bitter cry; and came even before the king's gate: for none might enter into the king's gate clothed with sackcloth. And in every province, whithersoever the king's commandment and his decree came, there was great mourning among the Jews, and fasting, and weeping, and wailing; and many lay in sackcloth and ashes. So Esther's maids and her chamberlains came and told it her. Then was the queen exceedingly grieved; and she sent raiment to clothe Mordecai, and to take away his sackcloth from him: but he received it not. Esther 4:1-4

Even Queen Esther was perplexed. All the favor she experienced in the king's courts had not prepared her for the reality of impending tragedy. Had she been sensitive to the need and in tune with the times, she would not have sent clothing to Mordecai.

Mordecai was taking the course that he knew had worked with his forefathers. He fasted and prayed.

It is like this with us at times. If our ear is not tuned to what the Lord is doing, we can miss it. Esther, the Jewish girl, now queen, was caught up in the affairs of the king's court, and did not even know that the lives of her own people were threatened.

We need to take care, in order to be fine-tuned to God's purposes. Here is where spiritual timing is so necessary; having an ear tuned to hear God's voice and also tuned to the signs of the times. Jesus admonishes us to watch the signs of the times *so we may know.* Esther was concerned with Mordecai's temporal needs and emotional needs. Now there is nothing wrong with being concerned with another's needs; we should be. But Esther did not consider the spiritual implications of Mordecai's behavior.

The Burden Of Prayer

Isn't it true that we can be quick to try cheering people up because they are not acting as usual? Do we even consider they are functioning within a spiritual realm of which we are not presently perceptive?

The burden of prayer (a prayer burden) is a most neglected area today. Our churches need prayer warriors who are willing to lock themselves in with God until there is a release within that individual's spirit in the realm of prayer.

What is a prayer burden? And what is intercession?

First, let us consider the prayer burden. When God the Holy Spirit desires to express His prayer through us, we may feel heaviness, even a sense of being depressed. We are burdened. We may or may not recognize the need; but if we respond to the heaviness by drawing aside to the inner chamber, a place of private prayer, the Holy Spirit will use us. The burden constitutes the unexpressed prayer. When voice is given to the prayer and it is released, our burden will lift and lightness will return. If heaviness descends again, we must resume praying.

To recognize the prayer burden requires spiritual sensitivity. Whenever we become aware of a sense of heaviness, rather than assuming we are "down in the dumps," we should seek to find a release in prayer. Many times we miss opportunities to become instruments in God's hands through prayer, simply because we, like Esther, are insensitive to the real need, the need to pray.

The prayer burden may also be felt and its release may be experienced in the public prayer meeting. But as Andrew Murray cautioned, attendance at a prayer meeting might be mere form unless time is spent also in the inner chamber.

Intercession

If chapter four of Esther says anything, it clearly illustrates the spiritual wrestling that takes place in the heavenly realm through the ministry of intercession.

We might distinguish between the prayer burden and

intercession by thinking of a backpack. When it is on our back, we are weighed down by the burden; the burden is relieved when we remove it. The process of unpacking the bag is intercession.

We notice in Esther 4:2, "[Mordecai] *came even before the king's gate: for none might enter into the king's gate clothed with sackcloth.*" Being clothed in sackcloth would bear the semblance of an evil omen to the king.

The customary sign of bitter grief was that of renting or tearing clothes, putting on sackcloth and sitting in ashes, or sprinkling ashes upon the head. This kind of grief portrays death and was used as a sign of repentance. Repentance is not preached today as it was in any of the great moves of God. *Genuine repentance is an ongoing spiritual exercise, and it becomes deeper as our relationship with the Lord deepens.*

In the tabernacle worship, repentance and death took place in the Outer Court. The holy place was the place of prayer. So it is with us today. Once we have repented of sin we have died to our sins or trespasses; then we may take our place of intercession in behalf of others, inside the gate, in the Holy Place at the altar of incense, *in the resurrected life and power of Christ.*

REPENTANCE IS THE GATEWAY TO POWER IN PRAYER.

Note that even though Esther was insensitive to the needs around her, God used her. Her availability and willingness, her submission and interest gained the king's favor at this time in her experience. She had some growing and developing to do, but she was willing.

We may not think we are much in God's eyes, but He looks upon our availability, not our ability. He will use us to the extent that we are available to Him. He will change us, teach us, guide us, and reveal His ways if we are willing to be taught.

Esther may have been too caught up in her own affairs to hear of the terrible plight of her people, but when she received the word, she was faced with the most crucial demand of her life. The process of purification to enter the king's chamber and all the times of intimate friendship that she enjoyed was about to be tested. Was her relationship with the king consistent enough to meet this challenge?

Mordecai tells Esther's attendant of the terrible death sentence upon the Jews and asks Esther to *"go in unto the king, to make supplication unto him, and to make request before him for her people"* (Esther 4:8).

The request was for a mediator, that ministry of standing in the gap to ward off judgment.

We find Esther's reply in verse 11:

"All the king's servants and the people of the king's provinces know that any person, be it man or woman, who shall go into the inner court to the king without being called shall be put to death; there is but one law for him, except [him] to whom the king shall hold out the golden scepter, that he may live. But I have not been called to come to the king these thirty days."   AMP

Mordecai's wisdom is seen as he sends his reply, *"What makes you think you will escape? You are also a*

Jew!" (See verse 13.) Then he holds out the bait: *"And who knows but that you have come to the kingdom for such a time as this and for this very occasion?"* (Verse 14, AMP).

Profound words.

For the past month, the king had not called Esther into the inner court. One day had followed another without the tangible sense of the reality of his presence. It was a dry spell. There were no goose bumps and shivers. She felt nothing. All she had was the memory of past times spent with him. But would he ever call for her again?

It is in times like these that we are spiritually stretched; they are the maturing seasons of one's spiritual life. If our hearts are bent toward carnal pleasures or self-satisfaction, these are the seasons where we are most likely to fail. But if we will tenaciously grasp and cling to the *fact of His Word* simply because *He has spoken it,* we will eventually pass through this experience to even deeper intimacy with the Lord than in times past. He has said, *"I will never desert you, nor will I ever forsake you"* (Hebrews 13:5, NASB).

Haman had given to the king a false witness concerning the Jews, and furthermore, he had bribed the king for the destruction of the Jews. He would get even with Mordecai for not bowing to him (see Esther 3:5, 9). So Mordecai, when he learned what was happening, went into the city in sackcloth and ashes and wailed loudly and bitterly.

The ministry of intercession is probably the most needed and yet the most neglected ministry in the Church today, as well as in our private lives.

"Men ought always to pray, and not to faint" (Luke 18:1).

"Continue in prayer" (see Romans 12:12).

"Pray without ceasing" (1 Thessalonians 5:17).

In other words, our life is to be a life of prayer. But there are those times when we are called upon to enter the priestly role of intercession for specific people, particular needs, urgent crises. When we submit to the spirit of intercession, the Holy Spirit works in us in an especially unique way.

The Spirit...maketh intercession for the saints (Romans 8:27).

Intercessors are chosen and are called by God. He uses a vessel to suffer the birth pangs of prayer to bring to birth His purposes in the Spirit realm. God chooses intercessors on the basis of their availability and willingness. True intercessors are not elected or appointed by pastors, elders, or church councils.

New Testament intercessors are behind-the-scenes, hidden, secret coworkers with the Lord, praying as the Spirit gives impetus. The Spirit is a Spirit of prayer. Intercession is not our work, but God's work in us.

Intercession is our highest privilege.

It had been a model marriage, one that had been held out as an example to others. Suddenly, it had turned into a nightmare of lies and deception because of a moral failure on the part of one. A separation had followed.

One morning, several months later, a young man (with a very limited knowledge of the situation) was in prayer when suddenly the Holy Spirit imparted a spirit of intercession in behalf of the wayward spouse. The intercessor found himself groaning and travailing with unutterable gushing as waves of sorrow engulfed his soul until he sobbed over and over in the Spirit, "Come home, come home."

Within days, the partner at fault called by telephone and pleaded, "May I come home?'

A period of restoration followed with spiritual, biblical counsel and submission to the disciplines of their local body. One day this couple renewed their wedding vows in a beautiful, Spirit-anointed ceremony. Their marriage has since stood the test of time.

This is the ministry of intercession in a life-or-death situation.

Esther was faced with a decision. Although she had been ignorant of the situation that faced her people, the Jews, she was shocked into reality as Mordecai sent the message to her that we find in chapter four. He said in effect, *"Your life is on the line, too, Esther, because you are Jewish"* (note chapter 4:14). He said, *"Deliverance shall arise to the Jews from another place; but you and your father's house shall be destroyed: and who knows whether you are come to the kingdom for such a time as this?"*

Esther certainly had something to think about. If she went to the king, she was subjecting herself to a penalty of death, for in verse 11 we read, and I paraphrase, "Everyone knows that whoever comes unto the king into the inner court, without being called, shall be put to death unless the king shall hold out the golden scepter." On the other hand, if Esther did not try to intercede for her people, she too would fall under the sentence of death that hung over the head of every Jew.

It was a sentence of death regardless of the course she took. I believe that Esther's spiritual eyes were opened at this point. When our backs are to the wall, we are many times forced to see ourselves for what we are. We are no different than Esther. She wanted to save her own skin, but she saw no way out. The Holy Spirit challenges us to risk our very lives, while Satan urges us to hold back part of the price. Ananias and Sapphira succumbed to that temptation and came under the judgment of God (see Acts, 5). Job, on the other hand, said *"Though He slay me, yet will I trust Him."*

Which course would lead to the greater, more noble death: Esther seeking to save herself, or Esther seeking to save her people?

Here is where Esther's character really radiated. The former years of teaching, the principles of her Jewish heritage, Mordecai's instruction in the ways of Jehovah—surely these were the teachings and the examples which now caused Esther to fling herself upon the mercies of Jehovah. See her reply: *"Go, gather together all the Jews who are in Susa, and fast for me. Do not eat or drink for three days, night or day. I and my maids will fast as you do. When this is done, I will go to the king, even though it is against the law. And if I perish, I perish"* (Esther 4:16, NIV).

Does it really pay to rear your children in the ways of the Lord? The devil would love to have every Christian parent believe his lies that many times are logical arguments with which he taunts God-fearing, sincere parents. Some of them sound like this: "If you force your children to attend church, they will rebel, they will tire of it and turn against it." "Just let your children make their own choices, don't try to influence them."

If we are not influencing our children, if the Church

does not have those moments of input, someone or something will. A child's mind and spirit is not a vacuum; and our children are being bombarded from all sides. So what will we believe? Lies from the pit of hell or the teachings of God's Word? The Bible says, *"Train up a child in the way he should go: and when he is old, he will not depart from it"* (Proverbs 22:6).

But he did depart, you say? Hold on. The last chapter may not have been written in your child's life.

Esther entered a period of life-or-death prayer and fasting. There are times in our lives when God intends for us to experience the intimacy of life-or-death intercession.

Some years ago, I was awakened in the middle of the night to pray for the unsaved husband of a Christian coworker. I had met the man only once, and in fact, did not know his wife that well. But I yielded to the presence of the Lord and found myself prostrate, in travail over this lost soul. For hours, I prayed in tongues for him.

The very next evening, my friend arrived home from work to find her husband, who had been a coarse, crude, God-cursing, blatantly vulgar specimen of humanity, now at the bedside on his knees crying his heart out to God, "Save me, please save me." He turned to his wife with tears streaming down his face, and cried, "I've just asked Jesus into my heart."

It was later revealed she had been on a fast. Her husband's conversion was lasting, and marked by a life of prayer until his home-going over twenty years later.

The fast described in the portion before us is referred

to as "the Esther fast." The Esther fast is here described as a three-day total fast. In other words, no food, water, or any nourishment whatever is to be taken for three days. The Esther fast is meant solely for life-and-death situations. It is not advisable to abstain from all food and drink unless the Lord initiates the fast. To fast from water could be harmful.

But what about those hopeless situations that may overtake us or those we love? Isaiah 59:16 reads, *"And He saw that there was no man, and wondered that there was no intercessor." May we take our positions as intercessors, even as Esther did, with the resolve, "If I perish, I perish."*

It may be a life-or-death matter....

10

The Golden Scepter

Esther 5

And when the king saw Esther the queen standing in the court, she obtained favor in his sight, and he held out to [her] *the golden scepter that was in his hand. So Esther drew near and touched the tip of the scepter.*   Esther 5:2, AMP

In times of spiritual crisis, that which has been wrought in our characters, the inward working of the Spirit, will be reflected by our stand.

Although she was queen, Esther feared to approach the king unless she had been called, but she finally made the commitment. *"I will fast and pray, and I will go in to the king – and if I perish, I perish."* The devil comes to us in a similar fashion. "Look who you are," he will say, or, "Your prayers will never be heard now. You don't know how to pray; you aren't spiritual enough."

All kinds of thoughts will race through our minds with one purpose, to keep us from a place of prayer and intercession. True, the Bible says that if we regard iniquity in our heart, the Lord will not hear us. But one simple answer for the sin question is the blood of Jesus, for the Bible also teaches, *"If we confess our sins, He is faithful and just and will forgive us our sins and purify us from all unrighteousness"* (1 John 1:9, NIV).

Our Father is rich in mercy. *"He who conceals his sins does not prosper, but whoever confesses and renounces them finds mercy"* (Proverbs 28:13, NIV).

Just as the blood of Jesus is the answer to the sin dilemma, so also the righteousness of Christ satisfies the demands of a holy God so that we may enter into His presence.

Esther told Mordecai that anyone who dared to enter the king's inner court without being summoned would be executed. The only exception was that the king hold out the golden scepter (see Esther 4:11).

Now Esther, after consecrated prayer and fasting, donned her royal robes and approached the king's chamber. *She knew how to come to the king.*

We may be trembling in the outer court because we have failed to recognize our King's open-door policy. We, like Esther, are still waiting for the King to call. May we firmly grasp the truth with which He would beckon us; the way has been made once and for all, which permits us access freely into the presence of the King. Oh the wonder of His grace, that we may come. True are the prophet's words that even *"all our righteous acts are like filthy rags"* (Isaiah 64:6, NIV). Yet we have been given royal robes because the scepter of His righteousness is proffered to us. Paul reminded the Ephesian believers, *"To the praise of the glory of His grace*

...He hath made us accepted in the Beloved" (Ephesians 1:6).

Here is a paradoxical truth. We may come boldly to the throne of grace (Hebrews 4:16), yet we must come through His prescribed means alone, through the blood of the Lamb.

> *But now in Christ Jesus you who formerly were far off have been brought near by the blood of Christ.*
> Ephesians 2:13, NASB

Esther was a beautiful woman and she had been subjected to the purification process. Still she feared. Even at our best we dare not enter the inner chamber except we enter under the divine scepter of the righteousness of Christ. Paul admonished, *"But put on the Lord Jesus Christ, and make no provision for the flesh in regard to its lusts"* (Romans 13:14, NASB).

Do we pray and neglect to acknowledge by what means we come for communion with our heavenly Father? Do we try to rush in and out of God's presence? If so, we probably have not left the outer court. Our Father's ear is bent, waiting to hear the whisper of His Son's name, waiting to deal with unconfessed sin through the blood of His Son. We may come freely, but there is a way to come.

According to Hebrews 1:8, our King of kings holds out the scepter of His Kingdom, the scepter of righteousness. It is His righteousness alone which clothes us and covers the shame of our nakedness, our exposed sin, in His holy presence.

Anyone who has traveled abroad knows the importance of a passport. You wait in an immigrants' line, to hand over that passport for examination. The immigration officer affixes the stamp of approval on one of its pages and you gain entrance to a foreign country. Without it you would be denied entrance.

Jesus is our passport to God's Kingdom and our visa to gain entrance to the Father's throne room at will because He made the way past the veil into the holy of holies with God. Esther drew near and touched the tip of the scepter. Oh the grace of God that allows my touch! I am that woman who pressed through the crowd to touch the hem of His garment. In turn, He is touched by the feeling of my infirmity.

Notice that the king asked, *"What is your request?"* (Esther 5:3, NASB).

Esther then requested that Haman, the wicked one, along with the king, come to her banquet.

Had I been in Esther's place, I would have gotten right to the problem. Isn't that how we usually function? We say by our actions, "Lord, I feel Your presence; now here are my requests." But Esther had already gained the king's favor. He was willing to grant her up to half of his kingdom. Now Esther said, "I want you to come to my banquet."

The attitude of her heart was, "I want to please you, my Lord. I want to serve you, to wait upon you. I want you to sit at my table and dine with me." Her action was in no way manipulative, for again, she had already been given assurance of the king's favor.

If he changed his mind (for her king, unlike ours, was unstable and impetuous), she was prepared to die. But first she would serve his needs.

How our King longs to be appreciated and ministered

to. How He looks forward to those times when we put our requests aside and come just to be with Him.

Esther had received wisdom. The days of prayer and fasting had paid off. Her spirit was sensitized to the king's needs and desires. Pleasing him was now first on her agenda. Her own needs were at the bottom of the list. Furthermore, she had been given the Lord's strategy for the situation. She would not only entertain the king, but she would invite the enemy right into his presence!

Whenever you bring the enemy onto the King's ground, the enemy will either show his hand or back off.

Esther's strategy was of divine origin. She was not now dealing with the enemy on her own terms. She had been on her face before Jehovah. There was no need to employ another's formula. No need for seminars and how-to books. Esther had been in touch with Heaven's hot line.

We may talk about authority and brag about our place, our position in the body or the gifts and endowments entrusted to us; but until we have been upon our faces seeking God's answer for our particular problem, the strategy will not work. Repeating pet phrases amuses and entertains the enemy. It does not drive him out. He loves our antics.

> *"If it pleases the king,...let the king, together with Haman, come today to a banquet I have prepared for him."*
>
> Esther 5:4, NIV

It is a good thing to get the enemy over to the King's territory, but only when you have been prepared with the discipline of prayer and fasting, and when you are wearing the whole armor of God described in Ephesians 6. The Lord gave Esther a strategy Jesus used many times Himself. There was that occasion when a man came before Jesus and knelt down and said, "Lord, have mercy on my son." His son was a mentally disturbed individual and apparently subject to seizures as well. The disciples had tried to heal the boy, but without success.

Jesus said, *"Bring him here to Me."* Jesus rebuked the devil, and the man's son was completely cured. He had called the enemy onto His territory. After this happened, the disciples asked Jesus, "Why couldn't we do that?" Jesus reprimanded them for their lack of faith, but added, "This kind does not go out except by prayer and fasting" (see Matthew 17:14-21).

We hear about the struggle that is often encountered when we take the Gospel into the streets, the parks, and other areas. It will ever be a struggle unless we carry with us the elements of a life of prayer, the kind we read about in the Acts of the Apostles.

When we invite sinners to church, we are bringing them into an environment charged (hopefully) with the King's presence; we seek to bring God's enemy into God's territory, a place of power. But please notice, the power is where God's glory abides; and His glory is resident in His presence. *Do we allow His presence a place of supremacy in our meetings?*

Prayer prepares us for deeper intimacy with God where He may reveal spiritual strategies for dealing with the enemy. But those who brag about their prayer lives have a missing ingredient.

HUMILITY IS THE GATEWAY TO WISDOM.

Notice the change that had occurred in Esther. See her trepidation when Mordecai suggested that she become involved in the problem. After all, this king had wasted no time getting Vashti off his hands! Esther the queen was transformed from a fearful woman who thought she was a goner, to a courageous warrior. Three days of fasting had changed her outlook. She did not tremble in the outer court. Neither did she charge into the chamber.

She drew near in humility.

In humility she touched the tip of the king's scepter, and now her courage is unprecedented as she lures the enemy into her camp! God has a strategy for every situation, and for spiritual warfare we need the mind of the Lord.

Haman was sent for, and as the three dined, the king again asked Esther for her request (see Esther 5:6); and again Esther invited the king and Haman to a second banquet, and added, *"Then I will answer the king's question"* (Esther 5:8, NIV).

Haman gloated over the invitation; *"I am invited by her with the king"* (Esther 5:12, NASB). But it galled him to see Mordecai the Jew sitting at the king's gate.

There are those who will never understand the Lord's favor upon us. They will be eaten up with jealousy just seeing us sitting in the King's gate. Like Haman, they would like to wish us away.

Haman bragged to his wife Zeresh and all his friends about the invitation he had received. As the ungodly

do, they gave him advice as to how to deal with
Mordecai!

> [They] *said to him, "Have a gallows built, seventy-five
> feet high, and ask the king in the morning to have Mordecai
> hanged on it...." This suggestion delighted Haman, and
> he had the gallows built.*   Esther 5:14, NIV

> *If he only knew....*

11

The Royal Robes

Esther 6

Let them bring a royal robe which the king has worn, and the horse on which the king has ridden, and on whose head a royal crown has been placed.   Esther 6:8, NASB

The divine arrangement of circumstances, which the Holy Spirit orchestrates, may be hidden behind the scenes for a time, but eventually the curtain rises.

Day after day, Mordecai had been faithfully at his post at the king's gate. He had been steadfast in prayer, and persistent in his refusal to pay homage to Haman or any other man. His trust and confidence was in Jehovah, the God of his fathers, and He alone would he worship.

He had assured Esther that Jehovah would deliver His own people, whether by her hand or by another. Mordecai was a man of faith. He fully believed in the God who had made a way through the Red Sea, that

Holy One of Israel who had thundered His commandments from Mount Sinai. Mordecai, who lived among those Jews who remained in exile, must have had a heart for Zion, the city of God.

In many ways Mordecai's role in the whole scenario can be compared to that of the Holy Spirit. It was Mordecai who had taught Esther, then led and directed her as she moved to the king's palace. Mordecai had watched over her and monitored her progress. It was Mordecai who protected the king by speaking to Esther about the conspiracy against him. It was he whom had imparted the burden of prayer to Esther. Finally, it was Mordecai who convicted Esther of her responsibility to her people as he encouraged her to intercede in their behalf. What a beautiful portrait of the Holy Spirit's ministry with each of us.

The Holy Spirit can be described as a divine vehicle. This divine vehicle cannot be "driven" or "used" by us —we are to be used by Him. He is the "motor," the power, the impetus behind the action. Honest acknowledgment of our own impotence generates His power. The Holy Spirit is therefore that divine vehicle of expression as we open our spirits to His working.

Basically, we are addicted to ourselves. Spiritual aspirations are placed within us, but many times we stand in their way. When I am freed from myself, His desires can be released in and through me. I am free, liberated by the mastery of Jesus. He binds me to Himself, but when He does, He sets me free. The ego itself, having been released, becomes a divine vehicle of expression. The Lord does not destroy my ego, but uses it to project the self-less Christ, to magnify Him. He must increase;

I must decrease (see John 3:30). This is true submission. In Him dwells all the fullness (see Colossians 1:19). God is full to overflowing, and He wants to pour into us.

The Holy Spirit also becomes our divine escort, ushering us into His expressions, gifts, and callings according to the will and purpose of God. The Holy Spirit is also the Divine Tenant, sent not only to abide in us, but also to change us from the inside out.

In many ways, He takes the position of the parent who follows the child up the slide and allows the child to sit at the top and look all around. Mom or Dad stands on the top step behind the child and hopes he'll decide to let go. But they'll never push. They wait for the child's decision; and if the child decides to back up, they'll get out of the way. The Holy Spirit is a gentleman, and He prefers not to force Himself upon us. Like Mordecai, He sits at the gate and watches and waits.

Now we read these words, *"During that night the king could not sleep"* (Esther 6:1, NASB). I believe it was prayer that caused the king's sleeplessness. Mordecai and all the Jews, and Esther and her maids had been fasting. God was moving into the situation.

Our King never slumbers nor sleeps, but is ever watchful, and leans His ear toward our cries. *"You who call on the LORD, give yourselves no rest, and give Him no rest"* (Isaiah 62:6-7, NIV).

The king gave an order for the book of records, the chronicles, to be read to him. What a coincidence that *"it was found written what Mordecai had reported"* (Esther 6:2, NASB). Coincidence? Isn't it strange that all this time had gone by, and the king had completely forgotten the incident recorded in chapter two, where

Mordecai had uncovered the plot against the king and had actually saved his life?

The king asked, "What honor or dignity has been bestowed on Mordecai for this?" Then the king's servants who attended him said, "Nothing has been done for him" (Esther 6:3, NASB).

Mordecai had not asked for a reward. He simply did the right thing. How different from the power struggles we see, not only in the world but in the Church as well. Sometimes we faithfully serve with little thanks, but we are not to be weary in well doing. All we do is to be done as unto the Lord; thus we leave the results to Him.

The faint-hearted are the enemy's targets. If we feel unappreciated for our efforts, we need to reevaluate our motivations and *redirect the enemy's darts back to him,* even as Haman's evil plot against Mordecai backfired.

The king asked his servants, "Who is in the court?" and it seems that Haman just happened (?) to be there. The divine arrangement was falling into place. "Let him come in," the king said, and Haman was sent for.

Whenever Satan has an audience with the King, it is a no-win situation for him. He tried it with Job, and he will try it with us. The Lord allowed Satan to test Job severely. I personally prefer not to experience what Job went through. Yet I know, because of the tests and trials that I have gone through, that I will overcome as long as I am trusting in the faithfulness of the Lord. Even should Satan seem to have a case against us, our beloved Bridegroom knows those who belong to Him.

The irony of God! The king asked Haman to decide upon the honor that would be bestowed upon "the man whom the king delights to honor." Haman thought to himself, *"To whom would the king delight to do honor more than to me?"* (Esther 6:6, AMP). Self-seeking power struggles have no place in the kingdom of God.

On one occasion, several of the disciples approached Jesus, saying, *"Who then is greatest in the kingdom of heaven?"* (Matthew 18:1, NASB). Jesus presented to them a child as an example of greatness. In Mark's gospel, Jesus questioned the disciples about their conversation on the way to Capernaum. They had been arguing about which of them was the greatest among them, but they didn't want to tell Jesus about their discussion. When we are walking with the King, we know what will displease Him. Why do we try to hide behind a mask of self-righteousness? Jesus said, *"And whoever exalts himself shall be humbled; and whoever humbles himself shall be exalted"* (Matthew 23:12, NASB).

When our King sees fit to honor one of His servants, there is no limit to the length to which He will go. Here is where some fail, for the King's honor is not intended to go to our heads, but should have its humbling effect upon our hearts. Haman's motives were wicked; he operated from a proud and boastful spirit born of Satan's kingdom.

A self-exalting spirit has no place in God's Kingdom. *"Let them bring a royal robe…"* (Esther 6:8, NASB).

Imagine Haman's mortification when the royal robes of honor, which he had connived for himself, were ordered for Mordecai. To his chagrin, Haman himself was commanded to deliver the royal garments to Mordecai and to lead him on horseback through the city while he proclaimed, *"Thus it shall be done to the man whom the king desires to honor"* (Esther 6:11, NASB).

On the occasion when the prophet Zechariah was given a vision of Joshua the high priest being accused by Satan, here is how the Lord responded:

> "'The Lord rebuke you, Satan! Indeed, the LORD who has chosen Jerusalem rebuke you! Is this not a brand plucked from the fire?' Now Joshua was clothed with filthy garments and standing before the angel. And he spoke and said to those who were standing before him saying, 'Remove the filthy garments from him.' Again he said to him, 'See, I have taken your iniquity away from you and will clothe you with festal robes'....'Let them put a clean turban on his head.' So they put a clean turban on his head and clothed him with garments, while the angel of the LORD was standing by."   Zechariah 3:2-5,NASB

When we choose to be on the Lord's side, even though we are not perfect, though we fail at times, the Lord looks upon our true heart desire. Esther donned the royal robe to approach the king. Mordecai was honored with a royal robe for his faithfulness and integrity. Likewise, when we go out from our King's presence with an assignment, we will be dressed in royal robes. But it takes the Holy Spirit to wrap the royal robe of righteousness around us. Nothing we do will cause us to deserve it. It is a matter of the heart.

Jacob was manipulative, a deceiver. His deception in receiving the birthright was uncalled for, from a natural perspective. But in his heart of hearts, he wanted that birthright, a spiritual heritage that meant little to Esau. God knows our hearts. The one most important thing necessary in order to realize the Lord's intervention in the affairs of our lives is the integrity of our hearts. A perfect heart in God's sight is one that desires Him, even in spite of weakness. The Lord can deal with your weakness. It is not a problem to Him. It is only a problem when we pretend to be that which we are not. Jesus did not have a problem with sinners, but rather with the self-righteous Pharisees and Sadducees. I'll never earn the robe that Jesus offers, but I'll wear it because He is my righteousness. He has intervened in my deception by insisting that I be honest with Him.

INTEGRITY IS THE GATEWAY TO DIVINE INTERVENTION.

Our King, our Beloved Bridegroom, adorns us with royal robes, for *"you are a chosen race, a royal priesthood, a holy nation, a people for God's own possession, that you may proclaim the excellencies of Him who has called you out of darkness into His marvelous light"* (1 Peter 2:9, NASB).

His mercy has brought us from rags to riches, but with the authority of the royal robe rests responsibility. Mordecai returned to the king's gate. He probably was surprised that he had been honored at all. Did he visit all his buddies and brag about the king's favor? No, he returned to his post.

Haman *"hasted to his house mourning."* When he told his wife and friends what had happened, his wise men and his wife answered with clear spiritual perception, for even the devils believe and tremble! *"If Mordecai, before whom you have begun to fall, is of Jewish origin, you will not overcome him, but will surely fall before him"* (Esther 6:13, NASB).

They should have thought of that sooner, for while they were still talking with him, the king's eunuchs arrived and *hastily* brought Haman to the banquet that Esther had prepared (see Esther 6:14).

Guess who was in the house....

12

King in the House

Esther 7

"Will he even assault the queen with me in the house?"
Esther 7:8b, NASB

God is always on schedule. We may think He has forgotten our requests or that He has not heard our
prayers; but when His arrangements are in order, the
move is on. His timing is perfect.

*"So the king and Haman came to dine with Esther the
queen. And the king said again to Esther on the second
day…, What is your petition, Queen Esther? It shall be
granted."* Esther 7:1-2, AMP

By the time we reach chapter seven, we have come
full circle, from feasting to fasting to feasting. It is well
to remember that the king may start with a feast, but

the order for us should be from fasting to feasting. We usually get it backwards: We start with a big pig-out to prepare for the horrible fast of one or two meals that we try to survive.

The successful fast is one that is linked to a God-given prayer burden, for then it becomes almost impossible to eat a meal. As our times with the Lord increase, He will impose fasts upon us, which will bring pleasure. The gorged stomach leaves little room for the exercise of the Spirit. When we enter the prayer closet with an empty stomach, the Holy Spirit is uninhibited. Likewise, I have found that entering into worship with an empty stomach will give the Holy Spirit Himself, freer access for expression.

It is not by accident that Jesus said, referring to the Old Testament, *"Man shall not live by bread alone, but by every word that proceedeth out of the mouth of God"* (Matthew 4:4; see Deuteronomy 8:3). The Holy Spirit stirs each creative word imparted to us. Thus Jesus described this activity of the Spirit as a well of water within us (see John 4), for He said *"out of his belly shall flow rivers of living water"* (John 7:38).

One more thought about fasting: From Isaiah, 58, we learn what the Lord's fast really requires of us. *"Is not this the fast that I have chosen? To loose the bands of wickedness, to undo the heavy burdens, and to let the oppressed go free, and that ye break every yoke? Is it not to deal thy bread to the hungry, and that thou bring the poor that are cast out to thy house? when thou seest the naked, that thou cover him; and that thou hide not thyself from thine own flesh?"*

Through personal experiences, I have recently been

given a new understanding of this text. We all agree that fasting is to abstain from that which is pleasing to us. We apply that premise primarily to food, although some have recognized that giving up TV or other such pastimes could meet the criteria. As a leader in the local church that I attend, it is my responsibility to visit those who are in the hospital or are house-bound, and to extend hospitality, to open my humble dwelling when it is needful. These are not graces that come easy for me. At times I really struggled with these issues, until I realized that these very acts are a form of fasting for me. Yes, it is still a sacrifice for me, but the struggle has gone because I realize that I am keeping the fast that is required of me.

What are those acts of kindness that are difficult for you to perform? Do them as a fast unto the Lord and they just may become your delight.

Queen Esther had exercised wisdom, divine wisdom; and moving in the authority afforded her, she catered to the king and to the enemy, Haman. The tables were to be turned, but Esther had no way of knowing the outcome.

"If I perish, I perish."

She did not realize her appointment in the kingdom was providential. Now she finally unburdened her heart to the king: "We are sold, I and my people, to be destroyed, slain, and wiped out of existence! But...*our affliction is not to be compared with the damage this will do to the king*" (Esther 7:4, AMP).

One of the most powerful prayers that can be prayed is, "For Your own name's sake, Lord."

Esther's cry, similar to Isaiah's, *"Woe is me! For I*

am undone" (see Isaiah 6) goes a step further. She stands between the king and the annihilation of her people, but she appeals to the king on the basis of what it will do to him.

Only that authority of those who wear the royal robes is recognized.

After the Israelites had made the golden calf, Moses prayed in effect, "Lord, the Egyptians will laugh at us if you destroy Your people now. After all, You swore by Yourself" (see Exodus 32). Elijah used the same approach in his contest with Ahab. He prayed, "Lord, let these people know who You really are!" (see 1 Kings 18).

Esther recognized the authority of the king's name and presented her request with integrity. She did not emphasize the robes of royalty she wore. The mask was off. Her true identity was known. She had nothing to hide now and nothing to lose, because she herself had become as nothing.

Abandoned to her God and in turn absorbed by Him.

When an Old Testament Israelite brought his burnt offering to the door of the tabernacle, he put his hand upon the head of the animal to be offered. It was a mark of identification, as the animal became his substitute. Jesus took a basin and a towel and identified Himself with us as a servant, then became our substitute upon Calvary's cross. When Esther admitted her identity, she forever sealed her destiny. She was willing to become a corn of wheat that falls into the ground and dies (see John 12:24).

The king's response to her was not anticipated. He was incensed. He said, in effect, "You tell me who has put you through this anguish, and I'll take care of him.

I'll take him into my woodshed!" Visualize Haman trying to crawl into the woodwork as the question hangs in the atmosphere: "Whodunit?"

Haman was seated in the king's presence, his sin uncovered. He became terrified, and rightly so. The king was so angry he went into the palace garden, perhaps to blow off steam, and while he was gone Haman used the occasion to try to appease Esther. He may have been begging for mercy, for when the king returned to the room, he found Haman *"falling on the couch where Esther was"* (Esther 7:8, NASB). The inference is obvious.

It was all over for Haman. The king was furious. "Will he even assault the queen with me in the house?"

The king was in the house! Paul wrote that our bodies are the temples of the Holy Ghost. Christ indwells us. *The King is in the house,* and when the King is in the house, the enemy's assault will evoke His anger. Not a fit of anger, but purposeful, decisive action born of divine justice.

Jesus stormed through the temple courts upsetting the tables where mercenary practices corrupted God's house. *"My house shall be called the house of prayer,"* He cried (Matthew 21:13). The King was in the house!

There is a story of an elderly, godly, praying woman, who admitted a young man to her apartment only to find he was there with devious intent. He was a burglar. But the King was in the house, and before long, the puzzled burglar was handing over his pistol to the feisty little lady.

There is a king in every household. Be sure that the King of kings is in your house.

"As the word went out of the king's mouth, they covered

Haman's face" (Esther 7:8, NASB). The Word, a creative Word, is a Word of power. His Word will not return empty, void. It will accomplish that which pleases Him (see Isaiah 55:11).

Again, the divine arrangement unfolded when one of the king's eunuchs mentioned there happened to be the gallows which Haman had prepared for Mordecai.

> *And the king said, "Hang him on it! So they hanged Haman on the gallows which he had prepared for Mordecai, and the king's anger subsided.*
>
> Esther 7:9-10, NASB

Our King is aware of the injustices that befall His children, His servants, His redeemed Bride. We may grow weary of struggles and think our sufferings are unnoticed. But our King wants us to react to our problems with trust and allow the changes He desires to make inwardly.

The true sailor gets as much enjoyment out of sailing his boat as in reaching the destination. The challenges of the winds and waves provide his thrills. Our journey to Heaven is not an easy pathway, but the truths to be discovered and the spiritual lessons learned are delights along the way.

Our bodies are temples of the Holy Spirit, a habitation for God. The Lord longs for those times of sweet fellowship with us. He is seeking, ever searching for those hearts that welcome and revere His presence. It is one thing to come to His chambers, but quite another to open the inner chambers of our spirits to Him. *"Where will My resting place be?"* (Isaiah 66:1, NIV).

SURRENDER IS THE GATEWAY TO THE OVERCOMING LIFE

Just as we value the revelation of His presence, our Lord will appreciate our transparency with Him. When our spirits are continually swept out and our lives surrendered to Him, when we are sold out as love-slaves, then He will have a habitation within us.

Our King wants to be welcome in the house at any time.

Have we dined with Him lately? Is ours a habitation in which He may commune with us, dine with us, and perhaps rest a while? Remember, whenever the King comes to dine, He will expect our requests.

He will notice what is most important to us....

13

In the King's Service

Esther 8

For the Jews there was light and gladness and joy and honor. Esther 8:16, NASB

The movement in this chapter is from intercession, to mediation, to deliverance.

Esther was standing on the threshold of new vistas in her royal role as queen. Her true identity and her relationship to Mordecai had been disclosed. They were Jews.

It was Haman's execution day. He was hanged on the very gallows he had intended for Mordecai. Haman's estate was given to Queen Esther and Mordecai was given Haman's signet ring, a symbol of authority in the king's realm.

Once again, Esther demonstrates the submissive spirit that so characterized her as she fell at the king's feet and wept for the plight of her people. She was a picture of Mary with her alabaster box containing precious ointment, a symbol of washing her Master's feet with her tears. She was a reminder of Ruth, covered at the feet of Boaz.

Notice that Queen Esther had first identified with the need; then she was used by Jehovah as an instrument of deliverance. Once again, the king extended the golden scepter, signifying her acceptance in his presence.

So Esther arose and stood before the king.

Her petition to have the king reverse his previous decree was unheard of. Normally, the laws of the Medes and Persians were unchangeable. But Esther had already seen the miracle-working power of Jehovah. She was not to be stopped now. Her faith was at its peak.

She was now moving beyond intercession and into the ministry of mediation. She echoed Abraham who had plea-bargained with God for the sake of Lot (see Genesis 18); she emulated Joseph who brought salvation to his father's house; she was Moses in the courts of Pharaoh. She little knew how close to Jehovah's heart she had grown.

For how can I bear to see disaster fall on my people? How can I bear to see the destruction of my family?
Esther 8:6, NIV

O Jerusalem, Jerusalem,... how often I have longed to gather your children together, as a hen gathers her chicks under her wings. Luke 13:34, NIV

And the king replied, *"Now write another decree in the king's name in behalf of the Jews as seems best to you, and seal it with the king's signet ring — for no document written in the king's name and sealed with his ring can be revoked"* (Esther 8:8, NIV). The edicts were scripted in every language represented in the various races of people so that everyone could read and understand. God communicates to us in our own language. There is no child too young, or adult too limited to understand God's speech when He speaks to him. When I worked in the mental health/retardation field, I witnessed first-hand the uncanny ability of those who were seemingly mentally deficient, to know or understand when the Lord drew near. One seriously disabled child who was dying from leukemia began telling me about the resurrection from the dead. From a natural standpoint she did not have the capacity to comprehend what came out of her mouth. Yet she knew because the Lord had spoken to her.

The writing in essence defended the lives of the Jews in every situation. They were given permission to annihilate any and all people who might attack them. They were now under the king's protection.

"There is one God, and one mediator between God and men, the man Christ Jesus" (1 Timothy 2:5). Just as Esther stood between the Jews and the king's original edict, Jesus is the bridge that closes the gap between us who face eternal damnation, and God the righteous judge.

Deliverance was fully provided for the Jews if they chose to accept it. So it is that our deliverance is complete. When Jesus hung on the cross, He cried, *"It is finished."* He trampled through hell's fires taking captivity captive, and entered His Father's Kingdom from whence He had come. He sprinkled His blood over all the vessels in the heavenly sanctuary, and therefore we are free. No longer need we be in bondage, slaves to sin. He penned our redemption with His blood of the new covenant and sealed it by His Spirit.

The day Jesus was crucified darkness loomed in the eastern sky, but in the dawning of resurrection power, the Lord Jesus Christ conquered death, hell, and the grave.

When we are cooperating with the Lord's purposes, we find He can reverse the situations that Satan has brought into our lives. Our King desires to hand back to us the house that Satan has tried to exploit.

Paul wrote, *"Therefore, my dear brothers, stand firm. Let nothing move you, always give yourselves fully to the work of the Lord, because you know that your labor in the Lord is not in vain"* (1 Corinthians 15:58, NIV).

In John 14, Jesus affirmed that He Himself would prepare a place for us in His Father's house. And Paul's words to the believers at Rome should comfort and strengthen each of us: *"I consider that our present sufferings are not worth comparing with the glory that will be revealed in us. The creation waits in eager expectation for the sons of God to be revealed"* (Romans 8:18-19, NIV).

If we are faithful, there will come a day when we shall be revealed. Let our faith be proved genuine, of greater worth than gold, that we may reign with Him who suffered for us. He is Victor!

"Behold, I am coming soon! My reward is with Me, and I will give to everyone according to what he has done. I

am the Alpha and the Omega, the First and the Last,
the Beginning and the End."

Revelation 22:12-13, NIV

May we submit to the Lord until we find within us a Mordecai spirit and the courage and fearlessness of Esther. May we find imparted to us the submissive humility and the quiet confidence with which Esther entered the king's presence. May we become intercessors and move to a place of mediation through the Spirit's ministry of reconciliation. Not through any goodness in us, but because of His redemptive blood and our standing in Him. He loved us and gave Himself for us. One day He will bring us, arrayed in fine linen, into the King's house and we will dine at His table at the marriage supper of the Lamb.

"Blessed are those who are invited to the wedding supper of the Lamb!"   Revelation 19:9, NIV

Our surrender to the Lord many times is temporary. The Lord is looking for our *abandonment to Him.* In the baptism of the Holy Spirit, the Lord has "moved into the house," and as He occupies more and more of us, we are conformed to the image of Christ. Our walk is progressive. Spiritual growth is certain as this abandonment to His will and His purpose in our lives takes over. Self-seeking and self-centered behaviors begin to drop off, like petals from a dying rose.

THE GATEWAY TO SPIRITUAL GROWTH IS ABANDONMENT.

Queen Esther had been granted her petition. She could be trusted with it. She was abandoned to Jehovah's cause. Such demonstration of faith and courage by one solitary woman now resulted in the deliverance of a race. The Jews were given permission to destroy, to kill, and to annihilate everyone who even smelled of trouble.

Again, Mordecai (that unassuming guy who sat daily at the king's gate, faithfully serving, praying, and loving) *"went out from the presence of the king in royal robes of blue and white, with a large crown of gold and a garment of fine linen and purple; and the city of Susa shouted and rejoiced"* (Esther 8:15, NASB). The whole city had been affected. You will recall that they were confused, "perplexed" by the king's previous edict. Now, Mordecai was avenged, his faithfulness was rewarded, and he was brought into the king's house in greatness. When we go out from the King's presence with an assignment, we will be dressed in royal robes.

The tables had been turned....

14

Victory and Promotion

Esther 9

> *Now in the twelfth month, the month of Adar, on the thirteenth day of Adar when the king's command and his edict were about to be executed, on the [very] day that the enemies of the Jews had planned for a massacre of them, it was turned to the contrary and the Jews had rule over those who hated them.*   Esther 9:1, AMP

Ironically, Haman had chosen the execution day by the casting of lots. Now the tables had been turned and the Jews had slaughtered their enemies. Even the princes and governors and "those who were doing the king's business" assisted the Jews because they saw how Mordecai had been avenged. *"Indeed, Mordecai was great in the king's house"* (Esther 9:4, NASB). Mordecai had been behind the scenes, watching and waiting at the king's gate; now he was moved into the house. The account reads, *"Mordecai became greater and greater."*

129

Some translations read, "more and more powerful" (verse 4). True greatness in the Kingdom of God is demonstrated through servanthood.

The disciples learned lessons of the Kingdom of God through embarrassing situations, and so do we. Like them, we think our so-called spirituality, or perhaps our good works, ought to give us prestige. In Matthew 20, Jesus corrected the disciples. First, the mother of the sons of Zebedee asked for a place of honor for them. The other ten disciples resented it. There was a power struggle about to take place within the group. But Jesus called them to Himself and instructed them in the ways of the Kingdom. "Whoever desires to become great among you, let him be your servant."

Another point of interest is that the Jews did not take any of the spoil (see Esther 9:10, 15, 16) even though they had been given permission to do so (see Esther 8:11). Haman, on the other hand, had planned to take the spoil that he probably intended to use to pay his bribe to the king. Perhaps the Jews had learned a hard lesson. Sometimes it is safer not to mess with the spoil. When you go into the enemy's camp, take back what he stole from you and leave all else behind.

I have heard of instances where people have brought "souvenirs" back from foreign countries, placed them in their homes, and strange things began to happen. Some of those beautifully carved pieces of wood just might have been used in heathen worship or cursed. Don't mess with the spoil—know what is in your home and where it came from, tapes and CDs included.

We are engaged in spiritual warfare, and when we experience victory in any area of our lives, it is absolutely essential that we leave the rubble behind. When the Lord graciously brings deliverance over a habit, leave all traces behind. If we foolishly collect trophies, we may find ourselves entrapped once again.

The edict was extended another day so that Haman's original wipeout campaign was actually doubled by the Jews. If God were to suddenly vindicate the unborn babies who have been ruthlessly aborted, or to unleash His judgment upon our country for removing prayer from the public schools, the extent of the slaughter would be unimaginable.

After these events we have the institution of the feast of Purim, which is still celebrated among the Jews today. The word *Purim* signifies lots (pur), as in casting lots, as they did for His garment at the cross of Jesus. The festival called Purim is celebrated on the fourteenth and fifteenth of Adar, which corresponds with our month of March.

Certainly, there are those more qualified than I to discuss the celebration of this feast, but it is generally understood that annually, candles are lighted on the night of the fourteenth. The synagogue service is a memorial for the deliverance of the Jews in Persia from the destruction devised by Haman, and a tribute to Esther. The service generally consists of a brief prayer followed by the reading of the book of Esther, which is a jubilant, triumphant experience. In the course of the reading, when the name of Haman occurs, the congregation boos or exclaims, "Let the name of the ungodly perish!" When the reading is completed, the congregation cries, "Cursed be Haman, blessed be Mordecai;

cursed be Zeresh, blessed be Esther," and other exclamations. The festival is also a time for merriment and gift-giving.

The Bible itself tells us: *"So these days were to be remembered and celebrated throughout every generation, every family, every province, and every city; and these days of Purim were not to fail from among the Jews, or their memory fade from their descendants"* (Esther 9:28, NASB).

It was and still is an important day in the lives of the Jews. It has been said that the continued observance of Purim is a monumental proof of the truth and validity of this history, the book of Esther. One day the fig tree shall bear its fruit again, for if we Gentiles were able to be grafted into the vine, how much more the natural branch, the Jew (see Romans 11).

Then Queen Esther, daughter of Abihail, with Mordecai the Jew, wrote with full authority.   Esther 9:29, NASB

Esther, a proficient, intelligent woman, apparently endowed with and well-versed in organizational skills, demonstrates her gift of writing, and is privileged to work with her godly cousin, Mordecai.

God places within every believer natural endowments and spiritual gifts that may find their place in the Body of Christ, and through the anointing of the Holy Spirit, those gifts may be imparted to others.

For I [Paul] *long to see you in order that I may impart some spiritual gift to you, that you may be established.*
Romans 1:11, NASB

IMPARTATION IS THE GATEWAY TO ENLARGEMENT.

A personal experience may help illustrate this truth. A brother whom I regard as vastly beyond my level of spirituality once asked me for editorial assistance. After reviewing my revisions, he expressed his pleasure with them and suggested we pray. His prayer had a humbling effect upon me that I never will forget. He thanked the Lord for my gift of writing, then said, "Lord, I accept and receive the impartation of her spiritual gift and I thank You for it."

We may seem small in our own eyes, and that is good; however, we must not take lightly the gifts and talents He has given. We are to allow the Lord the privilege of imparting those gifts to others who are like-minded, and to receive impartations as well, as the Lord leads. Our scope broadens and our tents are enlarged when He controls and directs our lives.

The Jews established the custom of Purim *"for all those who allied themselves with them"* (Esther 9:27, NASB). The Lord will link us to those who may contribute to our spiritual growth that we in turn may be used to impart truth to others. We have a celebration that supersedes the feast of Purim. Each time we partake of the Lord's Supper, the ordinance of Communion, we *"proclaim the Lord's death until He comes* (1 Corinthians 11:26, NASB).

I saw heaven standing open and there before me was a white horse, whose rider is called Faithful and True. With justice He judges and makes war . . . He is dressed in a robe dipped in blood, and His name is the Word of God. The armies of heaven were following Him, riding on white horses and dressed in fine linen, white and clean. Out of His mouth comes a sharp sword with which to strike down the nations. "He will rule them with an iron scepter". He treads the winepress of the fury of the wrath of God Almighty. On His robe and on His thigh He has this name written: KING OF KINGS AND LORD OF LORDS.

Revelation 19:11, 13-16, NIV

Oh that the Church would experience victory to such an extent that each time we gather together as a worshiping body of believers, we would enjoy the rapture of an open Heaven. When the worldly spirit of entertainment is displaced, and pure worship ascends to His throne, He will come into our midst in the power and demonstration of the Spirit. The operational gifts of His Spirit will once again have freedom to heal the sick, cast out demons, and perform miracles that will promote His saints to heights unrealized in our generation. Lord, let it be so!

15

Conclusion

Esther 10

*For Mordecai the Jew was...one who sought the good of his
people and one who spoke for the welfare of his whole nation.*
Esther 10:3, NASB

Esther had started out as a simple Jewish girl, orphaned
as a child and reared by her cousin, Mordecai, who
proved to be a dynamic, powerful force of prayer and
faith, impacting Esther for the higher purposes of God.

Her upbringing reflected submission and obedience
as she passed through the days of purification. And
when Esther was ushered into the king's presence, he
took delight in her; she pleased him.

Queen Esther's concern for Mordecai was displayed
when she heard of his fasting, and here we note evi-
dence of a spiritual insensitivity, due perhaps to immaturity. But in spite of her fears, she met the challenge to

go before the king without being summoned, and to plead for the deliverance of her people.

As we follow Esther's growth and watch her spiritual progress, we can draw many parallels for our own spiritual walk with the Lord. For who among us has not shown insensitivity or immaturity? Have we not felt the tremors of Esther's fear, and for far less cause? Oh that we might learn from her example of trust and submission, her courage and selflessness.

In her relations with the king, Esther repeatedly used a phrase, which the New American Standard Bible translates this *way: "if it pleases the king."* Although Esther pleased an earthly king (for Jehovah's purposes), her demeanor in his courts is an example to us as we develop in our relationship with our King, the Lord Jesus.

In the last chapter of Esther, we again have reference to the greatness of Mordecai; for he was one who sought the good of his people and one who spoke for the welfare of his whole nation. Mordecai is here seen in another role—not the man at the gate, nor the one giving the cues, but now as one who is second to the king—representing a son among brethren. Our Lord Jesus, the firstborn among many brethren, is the file leader of our faith.

How our precious nation needs those with the spirit of Mordecai and the courage of Esther. God would move in power and demonstration of His sovereignty as He did in the past, and beat back the forces of hell, expressed by the immorality and the spiritual corruption that surrounds us. I pray we will rise up, an army of believers, and allow the Lord to captivate our hearts for His Kingdom purposes.

My prayer is that the book of Esther has been endeared to you as together we have traversed its pages and have gleaned precious truths to better guide us to the path of victory—*for such a time as this....*

This is the gate of the Lord through which the righteous may enter... The LORD has done this, and it is marvelous in our eyes!   Psalm 118:20, 23, NIV

For Such a Time As This

Penny Smith

Show me, Lord, the treasures that I've failed to see,
The hidden gems within my shattered dreams.
The fingers of my grieving heart reach out to You,
Releasing all my hidden, sinful schemes.
For times I've heard You call, and turned the other way,
The salty bitter tears now kiss my lips;
And yet the hopeful promise of a better, brighter day
Assures me that I'm here
For such a time as this.

To share Your cross, Your power
Is certain death, I know.
Surrendered self, now trusting in Your love,
That purifying power, pouring forth to me
Redeeming grace enticing from above.

Teach me, Lord, to stay within Your holy courts
Where mysteries of life and death no longer cause me pain.
Extend Your hand, Your scepter reach into my weakened will
And lift me to a place of greater gain.
Invade my darkness with Your light
And clothe my soul in robes of white.

I know my times are in Your hands when shadows hide Your
face.
I'm Yours to bruise, to heal, to hold, to kiss.
I'm Yours, my God,
For such a time as this.

Suggested Reading

Absolute Surrender by Andrew Murray

Broken Bread by John Wright Follette

Deeper Life in the Spirit, by Hobart E. Freeman

Following the River, by Bob Sorge

In His Face, by Bob Sorge

Practicing His Presence,
by Brother Lawrence & Frank Laubach

Radiant Glory: The Life of Martha Wing Robinson
by Gordon Gardiner

Rees Howells, Intercessor by Norman Grubb

Release of the Spirit, by Watchman Nee

Secret of the Stairs, by Wade E. Taylor

The Christian's Secret of a Happy Life
by Hannah Whitall Smith

Waterspouts of Glory, by Wade E. Taylor

Gateways To Growth

The book of Esther is a book for today. It unveils a clear path to the overcoming Christian experience, and offers lessons and insights to the Church for end-time ministry. The keys to personal spiritual growth presented in this text will unlock the gate to a deeper, richer, more intimate relationship with the Lord. And from that enrichening will emerge from the reader's life, the unique blending of humility and authority that so characterized Queen Esther in the courts of the king she served.

About the Author

Penny Smith, a free-lance writer and speaker, considers herself a privileged vessel of the Lord who has been "forgiven much." Her life was in disrepair through the devastation of divorce when she met the Lord at the age of 24. In spite of her misgivings, the Lord called Penny into His vineyard.

Since then, she has completed theological studies, has been engaged in a preaching-teaching ministry both at home and abroad, and has ministered on radio for over 20 years. She has served as educator and dean for Christian International extension Bible schools and is the coordinator for Pinecrest Correspondence School of the Bible. Her writings have been published extensively in Christian periodicals. This revised and expanded edition of Gateways to Growth and Maturity conveys the burden of Penny's message to the Body of Christ to launch out into the deeper truths of God's Word.

Order Information

AVAILABLE GATEWAYS PRODUCTS

Gateways to Growth and Maturity
Opened through the Life of Esther
By Penny Smith

Gateways to Growth Radio Broadcast Teaching Tapes
(Tape Lists Available)

AVAILABLE EYES OF FAITH PRODUCTS

CDs by Tina Luce

GATEWAYS
(A tapestry of instrumental tracks, narration, and the
combination of original songs and poems by Tina and Penny)

EYES OF FAITH

SONGS FROM THE HEART

Additional copies of this book or information on other
available products can be obtained by contacting:

psmithGTG@aol.com

or visit Tina's website at www.eyesoffaith.com

Penny and Tina are available for
Ministry in Word and Worship